101
QUALITY WOODEN
TOYS YOU CAN MAKE
BY HUGH M. RYAN & JUDITH RYAN

TAB **TAB BOOKS Inc.**
BLUE RIDGE SUMMIT, PA. 17214

FIRST EDITION

TENTH PRINTING

Printed in the United States of America

Library of Congress Cataloging in Publication Data

Ryan, Hugh M.
    101 quality wooden toys you can make.

    Includes index.
    1. Wooden toy making.   I. Ryan, Judith, joint author. II. Title.

TT1745.W6R92   745.59'2   78-26446
ISBN 0-8306-9830-2
ISBN 0-8306-1046-2 pbk.

Contents

Preface

If your kids have been complaining lately that they are tired of playing with the same old store bought toys and games, perhaps this book can help you keep them happy and satisfied. Our book tells you how to build wooden toys and games for children. Chapter 1 covers the kinds of tools and wood that will be needed. Other chapters describe specific toys and games, materials required to build each one, and the actual construction processes. Among the toys included are various animals, cars, trucks, doll playthings, airplanes, boats, trains, rockers, house appliances (stove, refrigerator, etc.), puzzles and useful items like bookends and a clothes stand.

We have tried to keep the directions as simple as possible. The toys are not difficult to build; in fact, we think you will find it fun. Many diagrams and photographs are included to assist you.

We would like to thank all those who helped by offering suggestions. Our special thanks go to Kevin Kilpatrick for taking the photographs.

Finally, for our readers, good luck with your toy building. We sincerely hope that you and your kids enjoy the finished products.

Hugh and Judith Ryan

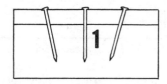

Working With Wood

Many children's playthings can be made out of wood. Wood is a versatile and useful resource which should be recycled whenever possible for conservation purposes. Woodworking is one of the oldest crafts known to man. A popular myth is that woodworking is extremely difficult. In reality, almost anyone can make beautiful objects out of wood by merely following directions carefully and using a little common sense. Wooden toys and games will delight your children and give you the satisfaction of knowing that you can create nice wooden items with minimal effort.

You can build most of the toys in this book with a minimum of woodworking knowledge, skill and tools. Some of them are so simple to build that you should be able to make them easily even if you have never worked with wood before. Others do require experience but are not hard. This chapter will give you an introduction to the woodworking process. Topics discussed include the types of wood to be used, required tools, finishing tips, procedures on enlarging cutting patterns and a way to make wheels.

WOOD

We recommend either white pine or plywood for all the toys. Both are relatively inexpensive and readily available. Most of the projects in this book need only a few small pieces of wood. So, it would be to your advantage to buy the discounted scraps available at most lumberyards, rather than the more expensive full-size boards and sheets.

White Pine

White pine is sold in a wide variety of sizes. It is easy to work, and looks well painted or finished naturally. There are two basic types of white pine—select and common. For toys, select is the better choice, as it is the

5

Table 1-1. This Table Gives Nominal Sizes of White Pine and The Corresponding Actual Sizes (Thickness and Width) In Inches.

Nominal Size (In Inches)	Actual Size (In Inches)
1×2	¾×1½
1×3	¾×2½
1×4	¾×3½
1×6	¾×5½*
1×8	¾×7¼
1×10	¾×9¼
1×12	¾×11¼
2×2	1½×1½
2×4	1½×3½

* Some 1×6's measure 5¼ inches, and others measure 5½ inches.

smoothest and has the nicest appearance. Within the select category there are several grades of appearance. "1 and 2 Clear" or "B and Better" have only minor blemishes, if any. "C Select" has a few small knots, and "D Select" usually is clear on one side of the board, but has numerous or serious defects on the reverse side.

White pine is sold by its measurements: thickness by width by length. However, the thickness and width measurements are names rather than specific measurements. We are all familiar with these names—2×2's, 2×4's—which really are the "nominal size" of the wood. The actual thickness and width are slimmer than the nominal size. Length, however, is always as stated. Use Table 1-1 to guide your selection.

Another quirk of lumber measurements is that ½ inch pine is actually ½ inch thick. Its *width* is a nominal measurement though. So 2 feet of ½ × 12 inches measures ½ inch thick by 11¼ inches wide by 2 feet long.

The most important point to remember when purchasing a pine board is to be sure it is not warped. You'll run into all sorts of problems if your board isn't straight, so check carefully before you buy.

Plywood

Plywood is made from a number of thin sheets of wood (veneer) glued together. It is sold in 4- × 8-foot sheets, and in the short ends department in 2- × 2-foot, 2- × 3-foot, 2- × 4-foot, and 4- × 4-foot sheets. It comes in ¼-, ⅜-, ½-, ⅝-, and ¾-inch thicknesses. Other thicknesses and panel sizes are available, but they usually have to be specially ordered.

There are two types of plywood—exterior and interior. For toymaking, the interior grade is sufficient. Plywood is further classified by appearance. Grades (N, A, B, C, D) stamped on the back of the plywood sheets indicate the quality of the front and back of the panel (Fig. 1-1). The letter on the left is the grade of veneer on the panel face; the letter on the right, the grade of veneer on the panel back. "N" and "A" grades are free from knots and plug holes. Use grade "A" for toys that will be painted, and either grade "N" or "A" for toys that will receive a natural finish.

Fig. 1-1. A typical plywood back stamp. The letter "A" is the grade of veneer on the panel face; "C" is the veneer grade on the panel back.

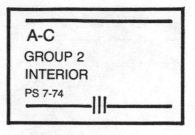

A-C
GROUP 2
INTERIOR
PS 7-74

TOOLS

To make the toys in this book, you will need a saber saw with an assortment of wood-cutting blades, a crosscut saw, a mitre box and backsaw, a curved claw nail hammer, nailset, small C-clamp, screwdriver, cabinet rasp, rattail file, and a ¼-inch electric drill with a depth gauge and an assortment of twist bits, spade bits, and hole saws.

Saws

A saber saw, or portable jigsaw (Fig. 1-2), is a power tool that can cut wood up to 2-inches thick. It works well on pine and plywood, and can cut both with the grain and across the grain. It can cut straight lines, curved lines, and can bevel cut as well. It can also saw out a piece from the middle of the wood. Purchase an assortment of blades with your saber saw—a scroll blade for cutting curves, a plywood cutting blade for plywood under ¾-inch thick, and softwood cutting blades for woods under and over ¾ inch thick.

The crosscut saw is a handsaw used for straight edge cutting across the grain. However, it works effectively both across and with the grain of plywood. Purchase a 10- to 15-point crosscut saw for a fine edge.

Fig. 1-2. The saber saw is excellent for cutting straight lines.

Fig. 1-3. This electric drill is effective for boring holes in wood. Hand pressure on the trigger controls speed.

The backsaw is a handsaw that has a rectangular blade with a reinforced top edge to keep the blade rigid. It is used with a miter box to make straight cuts and 45 degree angle cuts.

Electric Drills

A ¼-inch electric drill, preferably one with a variable speed motor controlled by pressure on the trigger, is a sufficient size for building the toys in this book (Fig. 1-3). You should have a set of twist bits in varying sizes up to ¼ inch, as well as ½- and 1-inch spade bits for boring larger holes in wood (Fig. 1-4). There are several accessories you will need for the drill as well. A depth gauge fastens on the shaft of the drill so you can bore holes to a specific depth. A countersink bit drills a tapered hole that matches the bevel on the underside of a flathead screw. Use it when you want the screwhead flush with the wood surface. If you want to make any of the toys with wheels, you'll need hole saws ranging from 1 to 2½ inches (Fig. 1-5). With any hole saw it is important that the larger the diameter being cut, the slower the drill should be turning if adjustment of speed is possible.

Nails

You must familiarize yourself with two types of nails to make these toys—finishing nails and brads (Fig. 1-6). Both should be driven below the surface of the wood with a nailset, and then hidden with putty or wood filler (Fig. 1-7).

8

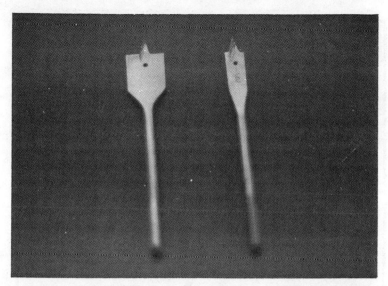

Fig. 1-4. These ½-inch and 1-inch spade bits are needed to drill larger holes in wood.

Use size 8d (2½ inches long) finishing nails for ¾- and ⅝-inch-thick wood, 6d (2 inches long) for ½ inch, 4d (1½ inches long) for ⅜ inch, and 1-inch brads for ¼ inch. If the nail is to be inserted within ¾ inch of the edge, it is best to drill a pilot hole for the nail. Use a bit slightly smaller than the nail.

For greater holding power, insert the nails at a slight slant either toward or away from each other (Fig. 1-8).

Fig. 1-5. An electric drill with a hole saw attachment is used for making toys with wheels.

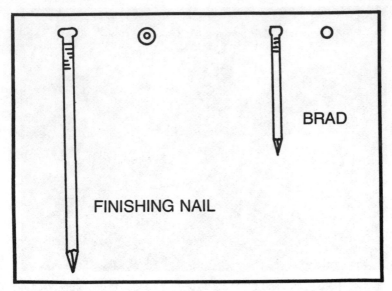

Fig. 1-6. A finishing nail and brad are the two nails used in wood toy making.

Screws

Flathead, roundhead, and panhead screws are the three types most often needed for building the toys (Fig. 1-9). Select flathead screws when you don't want the screw to show. Countersink the wood for the screw, and sink the head slightly. Cover the recess with wood putty. Roundhead and panhead screws are good for attaching toy wheels. Their decorative heads add a realistic touch to the wheel.

Screws are measured by diameter gauge numbers (0 to 24) and length in inches (¼ inch to 5 inches). The larger the gauge number, the larger the diameter. Whenever possible, select a screw length that will have two-thirds of the length of the screw in the second piece of wood.

Screws must be inserted in predrilled holes. The hole drilled in the first piece of wood the screw enters is called the *clearance hole*, and it must be the diameter of the shank or smooth part of the screw. The hole drilled in the second piece of wood is the *pilot hole*, and should be smaller than the thread diameter of the screw (Fig. 1-10).

Table 1-2 lists the drilling information for the three screw sizes you will use most often. In some instances, we have specified self-tapping panhead screws. These screws can be partially driven (like a nail), and then screwed.

All screws will insert more easily if you soap the threads of the screw beforehand.

Glue

A good choice is one of the liquid resin or white glues. They are easy to use, form a strong bond, and are quick setting. Spread the glue on both of the

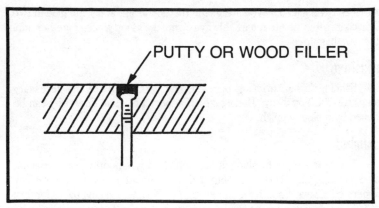

Fig. 1-7. Putty or wood filler is used to conceal finished nails and brads.

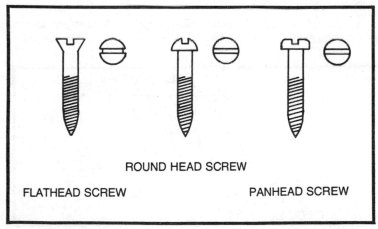

Fig. 1-8. Nails should be driven into the wood at a slight angle for a better hold.

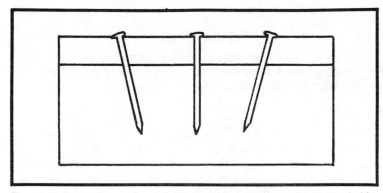

ROUND HEAD SCREW

FLATHEAD SCREW   PANHEAD SCREW

Fig. 1-9. Keep plenty of flathead, roundhead and panhead screws available.

11

surfaces to be joined. If you are gluing the end grain, apply the glue in two light coats a few minutes apart. Always clamp the glued pieces together until the glue has dried.

FINISHING

Sanding, filling, priming, painting, and varnishing are the necessary steps for finishing a toy. Don't take any shortcuts. The finest toy can be ruined by a sloppy finish.

SANDING

The first step in finishing is sanding the toy smooth. Use aluminum oxide sandpaper. Choose medium and fine cabinet paper to remove any imperfections and smooth the rough edges. Use fine finishing paper for final sanding before applying the finish. Always sand in the direction of the grain. Sanding across the grain scratches the wood. On straight surfaces, use a sanding block to prevent gouging the wood.

Filling

Exposed plywood edges have to be filled before they can be painted. Use wood putty or a ready mixed edge filler made especially for this purpose. When the putty is dry, sand the edges smooth.

Priming

A primer or sealer fills the wood pores to assure a more even final finish. If you are going to paint the toy, first brush on one of the many commercial wood primers available to seal the wood. If you plan to varnish over the natural finish, you can eliminate the sealing step if you use polyurethane varnish, which acts as its own sealer.

Painting

Acrylic paints work very well on pine and plywood. They are opaque and cover easily. If the toy is to be painted more than one color, mark the

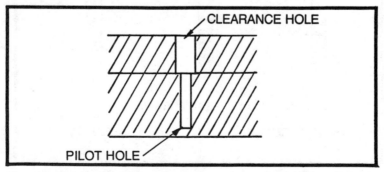

Fig. 1-10. These are examples of a clearance hole and pilot hole.

Table 1-2. This Guide Tells you Drilling Facts For Screw Sizes #8, #6 And #4.

Wood thickness (each piece)	screw size	clearance hole	pilot hole plywood	pilot hole pine
⅝ inch, ¾ inch	#8	11/64 inch	1/8 inch	3/32 inch
⅜ inch, ½ inch	#6	9/64 inch	3/32 inch	5/64 inch
¼ inch	#4	7/64 inch	1/16 inch	3/64 inch

areas to be painted different colors with a hard lead pencil. Paint the larger areas first, and then do the smaller details. Let one color dry completely before applying a second.

Varnish

Polyurethane varnish and acrylic spray varnish are the simplest varnishes to work with. Both give a hard, clear finish. Follow the manufacturer's instructions for applying the varnish. Sanding between coats is not necessary with either of these varnishes.

ENLARGING THE CUTTING PATTERN

Most of the cutting patterns in this book are smaller than actual size, and most are drawn on graph paper. To enlarge the pattern to actual size, draw a graph of squares the size specified in the cutting pattern. For example, if the cutting pattern states that each square equals 1 inch, draw a graph of 1-inch squares. Copy the outline of the cutting pattern onto the corresponding larger squares of your graph.

A NOTE ON WHEELS

Of course, the best way to make wheels is on a lathe. But unless you're a very experienced woodworker, you're not likely to have such an expensive piece of machinery. For the lathe-less, we recommend two different procedures for making wheels. One way to make them is to cut slices of wooden pole and then drill a hole through the exact center of each slice for a screw. A second method, and the one we prefer, is to cut out circles with a hole saw attached to an electric drill. You can quickly make absolutely identical wheels with a hole saw. What's more, the center hole is already drilled in each wheel.

The only problem you may run into with a hole saw is not having the drill square to the surface when the teeth of the saw start to cut. If all the teeth of the saw don't bite the surface at the same time, the resulting wheel will look lopsided. To avoid this possibility, first drill a ¼-inch diameter hole through the wood. Then insert the pilot bit of the hole saw through this ¼-inch diameter hole until all the teeth of the hole saw are resting on the surface of the wood. Then begin drilling.

Animal Toys

It's no secret that children adore animals—both real ones and toys. This chapter contains instructions for making various kinds of animal toys. Animal pull toys that move via wheels thrill kids to no end. The waddling penguin, seal and duck and the hopping bunny rabbit are pull toys that you can build easily. Make sure to have plenty of cord on hand. Of course, animal toys that do not move are also enjoyed by youngsters.

Also included in this chapter are directions for constructing the unique dinosaur toys. These prehistoric creatures are popular with kids; often the tots may have seen examples of dinosaurs on television cartoon shows like the "Flintstones." After finishing the animal toys, make a toy barn in which the youngsters can keep their new "pets."

SIMPLE ANIMALS: RABBIT, MOUSE, CHICK, AND LADYBUG

These four animals are a delight for toddlers, and couldn't be easier to make (Fig. 2-1). The five-to-ten age group enjoys them as well, if you make a family of rabbits, mice, or ladybugs. To make the smaller animal "babies," draw a ½-inch grid over the pattern, and then transfer the design to ¼-inch graph paper. Use the graph paper outline as a cutting pattern for the smaller animals. (See Figs. 2-2 through 2-9.)

Materials

For each animal, one piece of 1½-inch pine, at least 4 × 6 inches
yarn pompom for rabbit's tail
scraps of felt, vinyl, or leather for rabbit and mouse ears
tacks for rabbit and mouse ears
string for mouse tail
paint (optional)

Fig. 2-1. From left to right are a completed toy rabbit, chick, ladybug and mouse.

Construction

1. Outline the animal shapes on the wood. Use a scroll blade in your saber saw to cut them out.
2. Sand the edges smooth.
3. Drill a ¼-inch diameter hole through the ladybug for its eyes. If you would rather not paint on the ladybug's spots, define them by drilling ¼-inch diameter holes through the ladybug's body.
4. Paint or varnish if you wish.
5. Cut out the mouse and rabbit ears from vinyl, leather, or felt. Fold the ears in half lengthwise, and tack them to the heads.
6. Glue on the mouse and rabbit tails.

Optional Wheels

Use a 1-inch diameter hole saw attached to your electric drill to cut out four wheels from ½-inch -thick stock. Screw two wheels on either side of an animal with No. 10×1¼-inch panhead self-tapping screws.

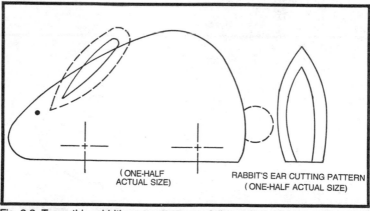

(ONE-HALF
ACTUAL SIZE)

RABBIT'S EAR CUTTING PATTERN
(ONE-HALF ACTUAL SIZE)

Fig. 2-2. Trace this rabbit's ear pattern carefully.

Fig. 2-3. A completed wood toy rabbit.

DOG AND PUPPIES PULL TOY

This toy is a take off on the classic duck and ducklings pull toy (Fig. 2-10). You can substitute just about any animal shape for the dog and puppies—cat and kittens, pig and piglets—whatever attracts your toddler.

Materials

2 feet of 1-× 6-inch pine
26 inches of 1- × 2-inch pine
2 feet of 1- × 1-inch wood strip
7 inches of ¼-inch diameter dowel
screw eye and cord
8d finishing nails
No. 10×1½-inch roundhead screw
glue
paint

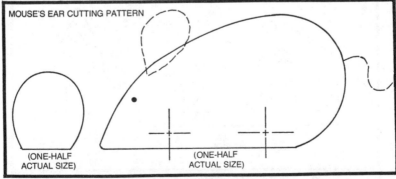

Fig. 2-4. Draw this mouse's ear pattern on the pine.

Fig. 2-5. A finished wood toy mouse.

Construction

1. Enlarge the cutting patterns for the mother dog and puppy (Fig. 2-11). On the 1- × 6-inch pine, outline one mother dog, four puppies, and four 1½-inch diameter circles for wheels. Saw out the mother dog and the four puppies. Sand the pieces smooth.
2. Cut the 1×2 into two platforms, one 8 inches long and the second 18 inches long. Round the corners.

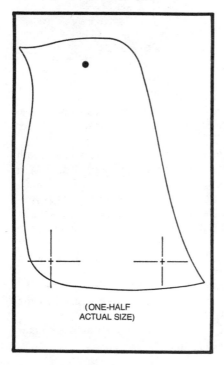

(ONE-HALF
ACTUAL SIZE)

Fig. 2-6. Trace the chick pattern on the pine.

Fig. 2-7. The completed wood toy chick.

3. Paint the dogs and the platforms at this point.

4. Nail the mother dog to the 8-inch platform and the four puppies to the 18-inch platform with 8d finishing nails. Refer to Fig. 2-10 for placement.

5. Cut the 1- × 1-inch wood strip into a 5-inch piece and a 19-inch piece. Drill a ¼-inch diameter hole through the longer strip, ¼-inch in from one end. This is the pivot hole.

6. Drill one ¼-inch diameter hole through the sides of each 1- × 1-inch strip as shown in the assembly diagram. Enlarge the holes a bit with a circular file so that the ¼-diameter dowel will be able to move freely in the holes.

7. Cut out the four 1½-inch diameter wheels from the 1×6, using a hole saw attached to your ¼-inch electric drill.

8. Cut the ¼-inch dowel into two 3⅜-inch-long pieces. Insert the dowels through the holes in the sides of the wood strips. Glue the wheels to the ends of the dowels.

9. Using Fig. 2-10 as a guide, glue the 1- × 1-inch strips to the center bottoms of the 1- × 2-inch platforms.

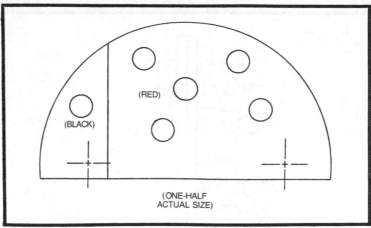

(RED)

(BLACK)

(ONE-HALF
ACTUAL SIZE)

Fig. 2-8. Outline the ladybug pattern on pine and cut out carefully.

10. Screw the puppies' wood strip to the mother dog's platform by inserting the No. 10×1¼-inch roundhead screw through the pivot hole into the 8-inch platform.
11. Attach a screw eye and cord to the front of the toy.

DOWEL PIG

A set of these whimsical animals is especially amusing, and very inexpensive as well. Use a mitre box and backsaw to cut the dowel pieces.

Materials

2-inch piece of 1¼-inch diameter pole
½-inch piece of ¾-inch diameter dowel
3½ inches of ¼-inch diameter dowel
felt scraps, string
glue

Fig. 2-9. A finished wood toy ladybug.

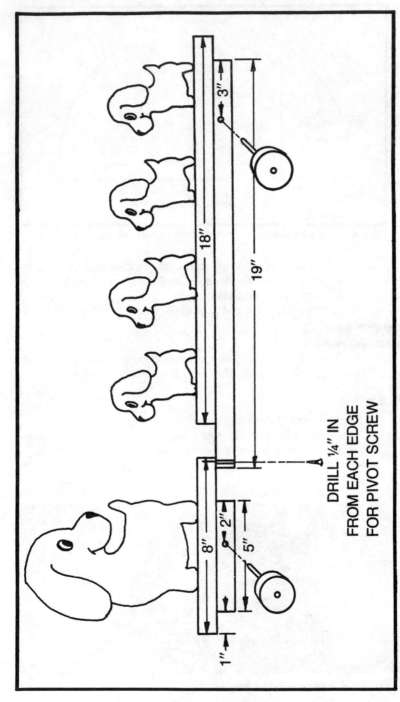

Fig. 2-10. Use this diagram to assemble the dog and puppies pull toy.

DRILL ¼" IN
FROM EACH EDGE
FOR PIVOT SCREW

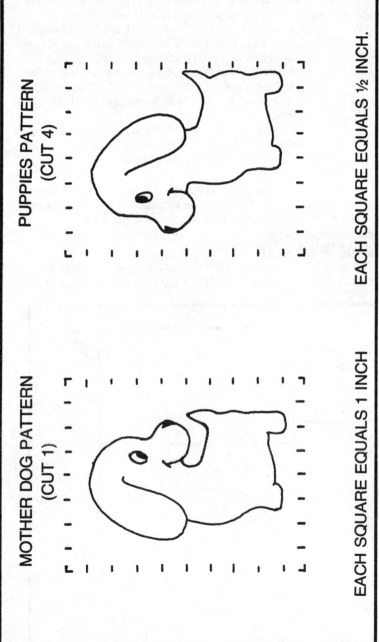

PUPPIES PATTERN
(CUT 4)

EACH SQUARE EQUALS ½ INCH.

MOTHER DOG PATTERN
(CUT 1)

EACH SQUARE EQUALS 1 INCH

Fig. 2-11. These are the mother dog and puppy patterns.

Construction

1. Glue a ½-inch-long piece of ¾-inch diameter dowel to the center of one end of a 2-inch-long piece of 1¼-inch diameter pole.
2. Clamp the assembly to your workbench, and drill a ¼-inch diameter hole through the center of the ¾-inch dowel (head), and ½-inch deep into the center of the 1¼-inch pole (body).
3. Drill four ¼-inch diameter, ¼-inch-deep holes in one side of the 1¼-inch pole for the legs.
4. Cut the ¼-inch dowel into four ½-inch-long pieces and one 1⅛-inch-long piece.
5. Glue four ½-inch-long pieces of ¼-inch dowel into the leg holes.
6. Tap the 1⅛-inch-long piece of ¼-inch dowel through the head and into the body so that ⅛ inch protrudes from the head to form a snout.
7. Glue on felt, leather, or vinyl triangles for ears, and a coiled piece of string stiffened with white glue for a tail. Draw on the eyes and nostrils with a black ink ballpoint pen (see Fig. 2-12).

ELEPHANT PULL TOY

The finished toy here is quite small (Fig. 2-13). If you want a bigger toy, enlarge the cutting pattern (Fig. 2-14). Trace the design on ¼-inch graph

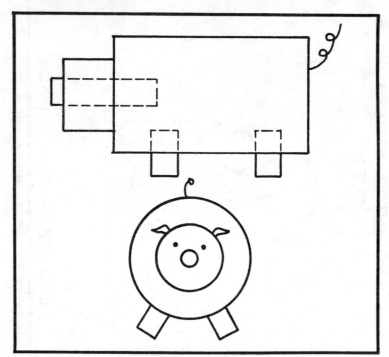

Fig. 2-12. Assemble the dowel pig in this manner.

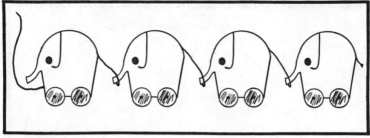

Fig. 2-13. These are examples of finished elephant pull toys.

paper, and then make a grid of ⅜-inch squares on a separate sheet of paper. Transfer the design from the graph paper to the ⅜-inch grid, and use the resulting outline as your cutting pattern. The wheel sizes and dowel lengths can remain the same. Buy 1-× 8-inch pine rather than 1-× 6-inch, and cut out only three elephants and 12 wheels.

Materials

2 feet of 1-× 6-inch pine
2 feet of ¼-inch diameter dowel
leather lace at least 23 inches long
small brass tacks
screw eye and cord
varnish

Construction

1. Outline four elephants and 16 1½-inch diameter circles for wheels on the pine.
2. Saw out the four elephants. Drill a ¼-inch diameter hole through each leg. Enlarge the holes with a circular file until a ¼-inch diameter dowel moves freely in the holes.
3. Using a 1½-inch hole saw attached to your electric drill, cut out 16 wheels.
4. Sand smooth. Draw the eyes and ears with a black ballpoint pen, pressing down into the wood to make a groove. Varnish.
5. Saw the ¼-inch dowel into eight 2½-inch lengths. Insert a piece through each hole drilled in the elephants. Glue the wheels to the ends of the dowels.
6. Cut the leather lace into three 7-inch pieces and one 2-inch piece. Tack one end of a 7-inch piece to the rump of the first elephant, and tie the other end once around the trunk of the second elephant. Tack the tie to the underside of the second elephant's trunk. Continue in this manner with the next two elephants. Tack the 2-inch lace to the end of the last elephant.
7. Attach a screw eye and cord to the bottom front of the lead elephant.

Fig. 2-14. Take pains when outlining the elephant pull toy pattern.

BUTTERFLY MERRY-GO-ROUND

As the odd wheel on the short side of the base moves, it rubs against the circle, which then revolves around the center pole (Fig. 2-15). Substitute angels for the butterflies for an especially nice Christmas toy. Planes and birds are good substitutions also.

Fig. 2-15. A completed butterfly merry-go-round toy.

Materials

1 foot of 1-× 8-inch pine
1-inch diameter wooden bead
1 foot of ¼-inch diameter dowel
3 No. 10×1½-inch self-tapping panhead screws
screw eye and cord
glue
paint

Construction

1. Using the cutting patterns in Figs. 2-16 and 2-17, outline three butterflies, one base, one 4-inch diameter circle, and three 1½-inch diameter circles on the pine. Saw out the pieces. Use a hole saw attached to an electric drill to cut out the 1½-inch circles. Sand the pieces smooth.
2. Drill a ½-inch-deep, ¼-inch diameter hole in the center of the base, at three equidistant points around the circumference of the 4-inch circle, at the spot indicated on each butterfly, and in the wooden bead. Also drill a ¼-inch diameter hole through the center of the 4-inch circle. Enlarge this hole with a circular file so that a ¼-inch diameter dowel moves freely in the hole.
3. Paint the different pieces at this point. Check the center hole of the 4-inch circle to be sure the dowel can move freely in it once it's painted. File again if necessary.
4. Cut three 2-inch pieces of ¼-inch diameter dowel. Glue one end of each piece into a hole on the circumference of the large circle, and the other end into a butterfly.
5. Screw the three small circles to the base so that two wheels are flush with each end of the 6½-inch side, and one wheel is in the center of the 3-inch side.

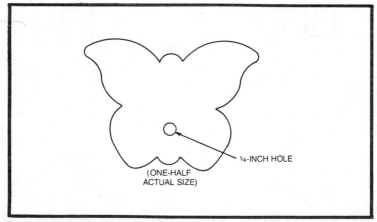

¼-INCH HOLE

(ONE-HALF
ACTUAL SIZE)

Fig. 2-16. Trace this butterfly pattern on pine.

6. Cut a 5-inch length of ¼-inch diameter dowel, and glue it in the hole drilled in the center of the base. Slide the circle assembly down this dowel so it rests on the single wheel. Glue the wooden bead to the top of the dowel (Fig. 2-18).
7. Attach a screw eye and cord to either 1-inch section of the base.

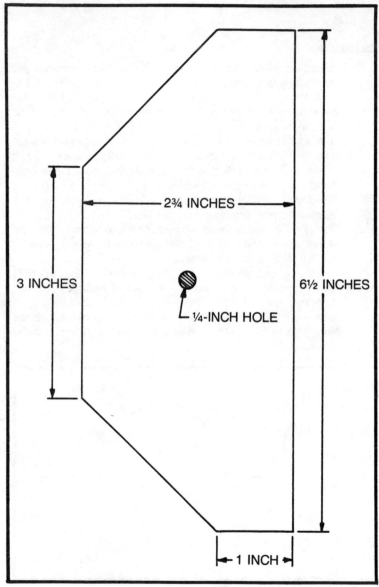

Fig. 2-17. Copy the base cutting pattern.

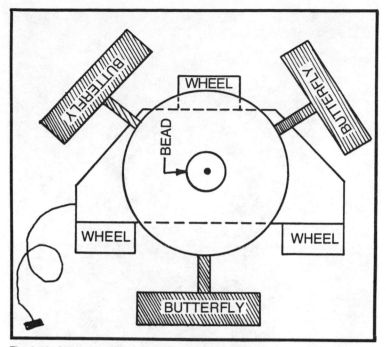

Fig. 2-18. Assemble the butterfly toy as illustrated.

THREE WADDLING PULL TOYS: PENGUIN, SEAL, AND DUCK

These three toys, with their off-center and out-of-line rear wheels, imitate the waddling movements of real-life penguins, ducks, and seals (Figs. 2-19 and 2-20). Compare these instructions with those for the hopping bunny pull toy, to be sure you understand why one toy hops and another waddles.

Materials

penguin—1 foot of 1- × 10-inch pine
seal—1 foot of 1- × 12-inch pine
duck—1 foot of 1-× 8-inch pine
In addition, for each animal you will need:
5 inches of ¼-inch diameter dowel
screw eye and cord
glue
paint

Construction

1. Enlarge the cutting pattern (Figs. 2-21 through 2-23). Outline it and four 2-inch diameter circles on the pine, and saw out. Use a hole saw attached to an electric drill to cut the circles.

Fig. 2-19. A finished penguin pull toy.

Fig. 2-20. A completed seal pull toy.

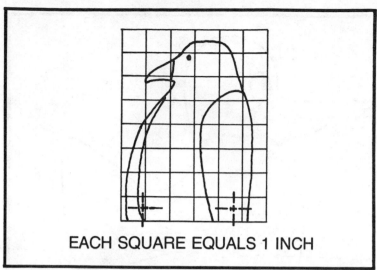

EACH SQUARE EQUALS 1 INCH

Fig. 2-21. The penguin pull toy pattern.

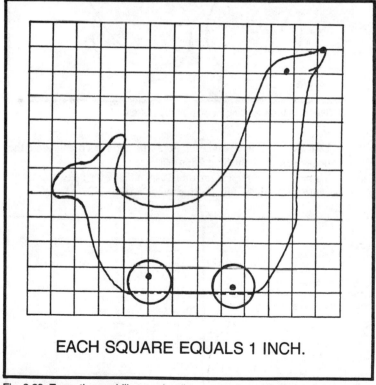

EACH SQUARE EQUALS 1 INCH.

Fig. 2-22. Trace the waddling seal pull toy pattern on the pine.

Fig. 2-23. Shown is the waddling duck pull toy pattern.

2. Drill two 5/16-inch diameter holes through each animal at the points indicated on the cutting patterns.
3. Through two of the circles drill ¼-inch diameter holes ¼ inch off center. Use these for the rear wheels (Fig. 2-24).

Fig. 2-24. Make sure to drill ¼-inch diameter holes ¼-inch off center through two circles for rear wheels.

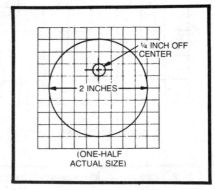

¼ INCH OFF CENTER

←—— 2 INCHES ——→

(ONE-HALF ACTUAL SIZE)

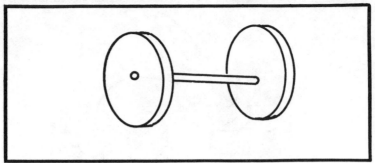

Fig. 2-25. Use this assembly illustration to fasten the rear wheels to the toy.

4. Sand and paint the animal and the wheels.
5. Cut two 2½-inch long pieces of ¼-inch dowel. Insert the dowels through the pre-drilled holes in the animals and glue on the wheels. Attach the rear wheels so that the axle holes are not at the same point in their eccentric orbit (Fig. 2-25).
6. Attach a screw eye and cord to the front of the animal.

HOPPING BUNNY PULL TOY

The rear wheel axle of this toy is off center (Fig. 2-26). This produces a hopping effect as the toy is pulled across the floor. Kangaroos, frogs, grasshoppers, and any other animal that hops can easily be substituted for the bunny figure. If you absolutely can't draw a substitute figure, use a simple coloring book picture as your cutting pattern.

Materials

1 foot of 1- × 8-inch pine
7 inches of ¼-inch diameter dowel
8d finishing nails
4 No. 10×1½-inch roundhead screws
screw eye and cord
glue
paint

Construction

1. Enlarge the cutting pattern and transfer it to the pine (Fig. 2-27). Also outline on the pine four 2-inch diameter wheels and one 2- × 6½-inch platform with rounded corners. Saw out the pieces. Use a hole saw attached to your electric drill to cut the wheels. Sand all edges smooth.
2. Drill two 5/16″ diameter holes horizontally through the platform to accomodate the wheel axles (Fig. 2-28).
3. Through two of the wheels, drill ¼-inch diameter holes ¼ inch off center. Use these wheels as the rear wheels (Fig. 2-29).

Fig. 2-26. The bunny pull toy hops because its rear wheel axle is off center.

4. Paint and varnish the whole assembly.
5. Nail the rabbit to the platform.
6. Cut the ¼-inch dowel into two 3½-inch-long pieces. Insert the dowels through the platform and glue on the wheels. In order for

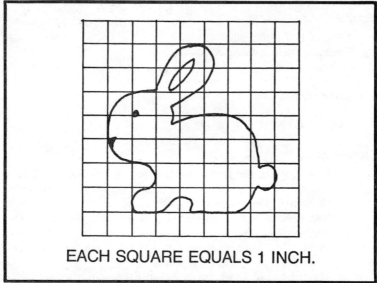

EACH SQUARE EQUALS 1 INCH.

Fig. 2-27. Transfer this bunny pattern to the pine carefully.

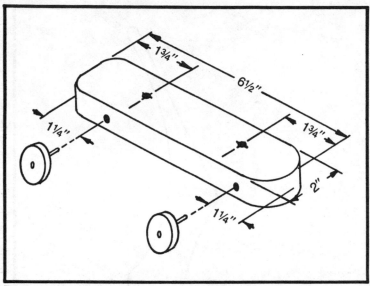

Fig. 2-28. This drawing shows where to drill holes for wheel axles.

the rabbit to hop and not waddle, the axle holes of the rear wheels must be at the same point in their eccentric orbit.

7. Attach a screw eye and cord to the front of the platform.

DINOSAURS

All children, at one time or another, become fascinated with dinosaurs. Our young son and his friends were entranced with these wooden replicas, and played with them by the hour. These toys are a snap to make; you can turn out an entire set in under an hour.

Materials

1. Pteranodon—1 foot of 1- × 3-inch pine
2. Trachodon—1 foot of 1½- × 10-inch pine

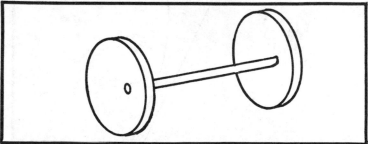

Fig. 2-29. Rear wheels have ¼-inch diameter holes ¼-inch off center drilled through them.

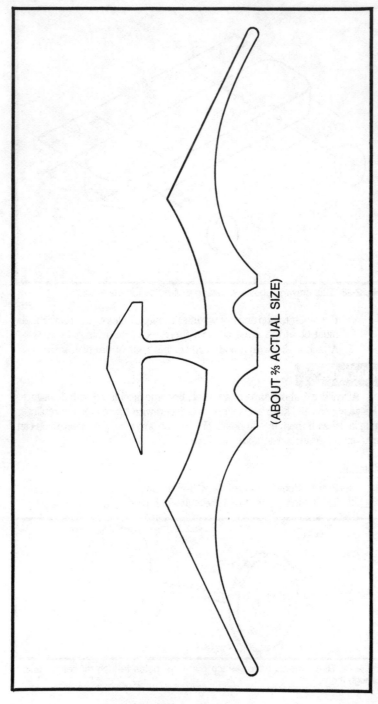

(ABOUT ⅔ ACTUAL SIZE)

Fig. 2-30. Remember that this pteranodon dinosaur pattern must be cut from 1-inch pine. (Note: This figure was reduced to 65% of its original size.)

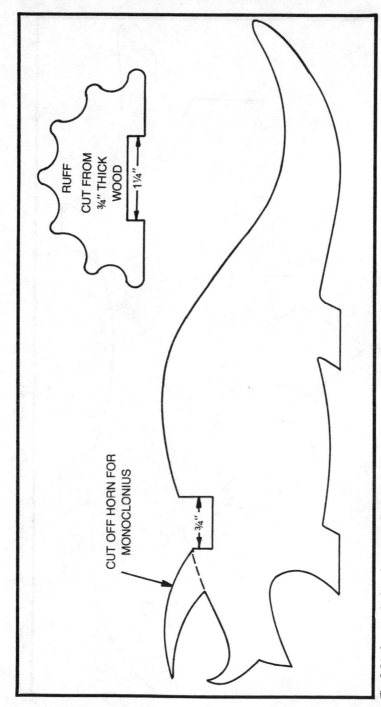

RUFF

CUT FROM ¾" THICK WOOD

1¼"

CUT OFF HORN FOR MONOCLONIUS

¾"

Fig. 2-31. A monoclonius-triceratops dinosaur pattern. Cut the ruff from 1-inch thick wood.

35

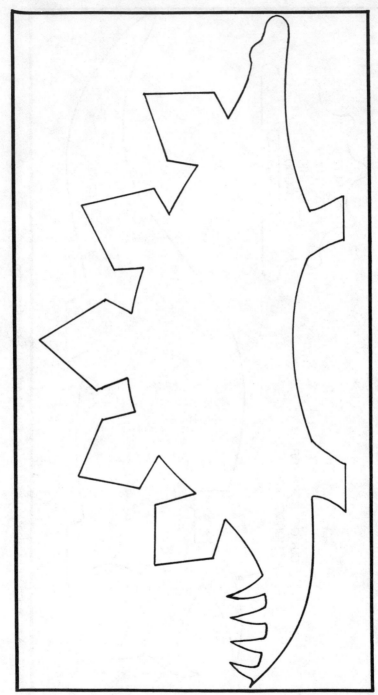

Fig. 2-32. Trace the stegosaurus dinosaur pattern on 1½-inch pine.

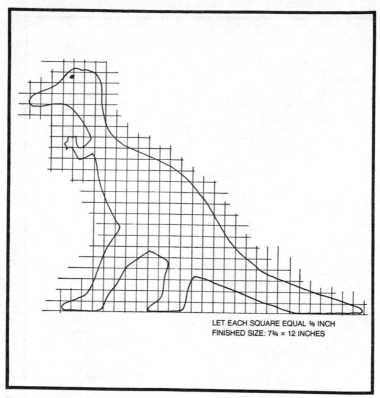

LET EACH SQUARE EQUAL ⅜ INCH
FINISHED SIZE: 7¾ × 12 INCHES

Fig. 2-33. Saw the outlined duck-billed trachodon out of 1½-inch pine.

 3. Tyrannosaurus Rex—1 foot of 1½- × 8-inch pine
 4. Brontosaurus—2 feet of 1½- × 8-inch pine
 5. Stegosaurus—1 foot of 1½- × 6-inch pine
 6. and 7. Monoclonius/Triceratops—1 foot of 1½- × 4-inch pine and
   a small scrap of 1-inch pine for each
   Dinosaurs 2–7: 5 feet of 1½- × 12-inch pine

Construction

 1. Enlarge the cutting patterns when necessary (Figs. 2-30 through
  2-36). Saw out the dinosaurs from the 1½-inch pine, with the
  exception of the pteranodon and the ruff of monoclonius/
  triceratops. Cut these from 1-inch pine.
 2. Draw on the eyes and any other features with a black ink ballpoint
  pen.
 3. Triceratops only: carefully cut out a ⅝-inch-wide space between
  the large horn to make two ¼-inch wide horns (Fig. 2-37).
 4. Triceratops and monoclonius: glue the ruff perpendicular to the
  body, matching up the notches in the ruff and body.

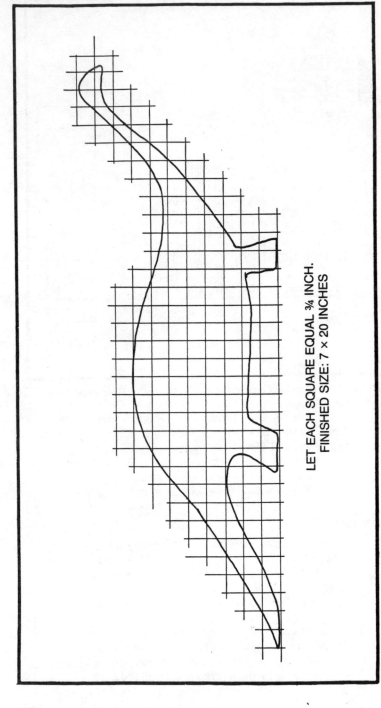

LET EACH SQUARE EQUAL ¾ INCH.
FINISHED SIZE: 7 × 20 INCHES

Fig. 2-34. Trace the brontosaurus dinosaur pattern on 1½-inch pine.

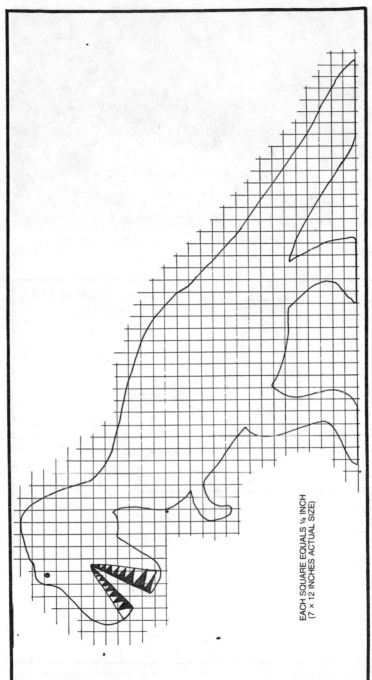

EACH SQUARE EQUALS ¼ INCH
(7 × 12 INCHES ACTUAL SIZE)

Fig. 2-35. The front part of the tyrannosaurus rex dinosaur cutting pattern.

Fig. 2-36. This is the back half of the tyrannosaurus rex pattern. Trace it on 1½-inch pine.

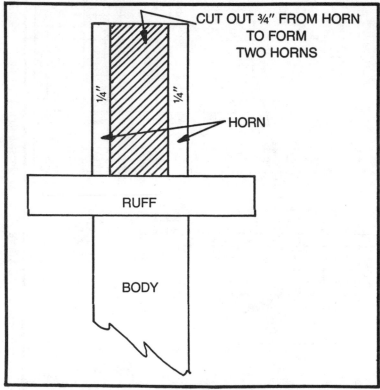

CUT OUT ¾" FROM HORN
TO FORM
TWO HORNS

¼"

¼"

HORN

RUFF

BODY

Fig. 2-37. For the triceratops, make sure there is a ⅝-inch wide gap between the large horn to make two ¼-inch wide horns.

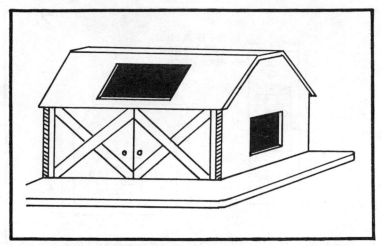

Fig. 2-38. The chick, pig and other animals will feel at home in this barn.

BARN

Of course the kids will need some type of building in which to place their toy animals. This two-door barn will work nicely. It contains two window frames and a hay loft. Paint the barn a bright color, such as red, to make it more attractive. Even Old McDonald would be envious of this structure (Fig. 2-38).

Materials

6 feet of ½- × 10-inch pine
two 3-inch pre-made window frames (purchase at a hobby shop)
4d finishing nails
four 1-inch brads
glue
paint

Construction

1. Using Fig. 2-39 and Fig. 2-40 as guides, saw out the following pieces from the pine:
   back—one 4½- × 9-inch rectangle
   sides—two pieces, approximately 7×7
   front posts—two ½- × ½- × 4-inch strips
   doors—two 3-15/16-inch squares
   center roof—one 4- × 10½-inch rectangle
   side roofs—two 3½- ×.10½-inch pieces
   loft floor—one 6½- × 9-inch rectangle
   base—one 9- × 13-inch piece.
2. Glue the purchased window frames into the window openings.

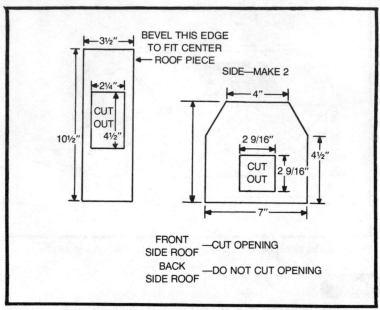

Fig. 2-39. Follow the dimensions in the illustration when cutting out the sides and roofs.

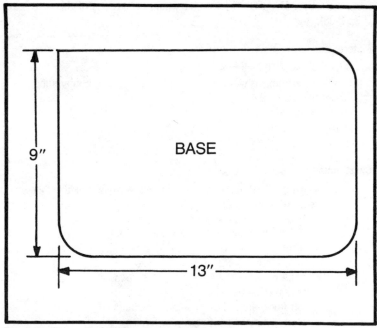

Fig. 2-40. The cutting pattern for the barn base.

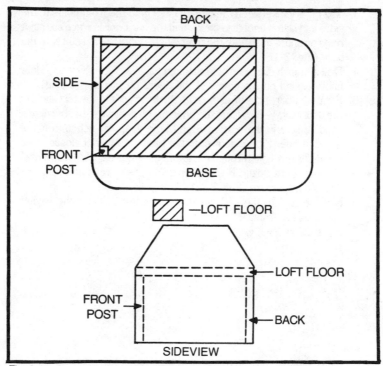

Fig. 2-41. Assemble the pieces as shown in these diagrams.

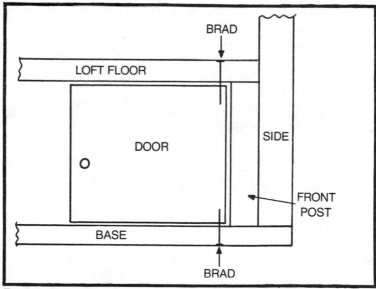

Fig. 2-42. The brads hold the doors well when inserted properly.

3. Nail the back between the sides. Then glue the front posts to the sides and clamp until dry. Next, nail the loft floor in place so that it rests on and is flush with the front posts. Glue the assembly to the base (Fig. 2-41).

4. Drill a ½-inch diameter hole through each door to serve as a door knob. Round off the edges of the doors on the hinged sides.

5. For each door, tap a brad through the base up into the threshold of the doorway, ⅛-inch from the edge of the doorway. Drill a corresponding hole in the bottom edge of the door, ⅛-inch in from the rounded side. Fit the door onto the brad, and hold it closed while you drill a tiny hole through the loft floor into the door. Drop a brad through these holes. If the door sticks, remove it and sand the edges a little more (Fig. 2-42).

6. Nail the roof to the barn so that the side roof with the hayloft opening is in front.

7. Paint the assembly.

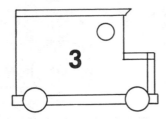

3

Cars, Trucks, and a Gas Station

If you are the parent of a small boy, this chapter should be required reading. Boys love to play with all kinds of cars and trucks. So, why not take a little of your spare time and build some wooden toy vehicles which will keep him and his friends amused? If you want to make all the toys described in this chapter, keep plenty of panhead screws close by for the toys' wheels.

We have included steps for building five 2 by 4 vehicles, two 2 by 2 racing cars, two 1 by 2 cars, a semi-trailer truck with three hitches, a basic truck and three variations, a delivery milk truck, and special vehicles like the tractor, steam roller and fire engine. You can even make a gas station so your son can pretend that he has his own business.

FIVE 2 × 4 VEHICLES

On the following pages are instructions for building a car, a van, and three buses from small lengths of 2×4's. If there's a new house going up in your neighborhood, you can probably obtain small pieces of 2×4 stud lumber just for the asking.

If you plan to make a number of wheeled toys, purchase a 4-foot length of ½- × 6-inch pine, and cut out all your wheels from this. Use a spade bit to drill the 1-inch diameter "window" holes through the 2×4. If you have an inexpensive ¼-inch homeowner-type electric drill, its motor will probably not be powerful enough to do the job. Instead, use a ½-inch spade bit and drill ½-inch diameter circles through the wood.

"BUG CAR"

Materials

> 7 inches of 2×4 lumber
> scrap of ½-inch-thick wood large enough to cut out four 1½-inch diameter

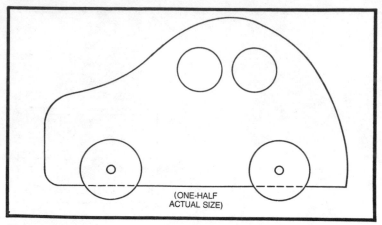

(ONE-HALF
ACTUAL SIZE)

Fig. 3-1. Trace the bug car pattern carefully.

circles
4 No. 10×1¼-inch self-tapping panhead screws

Construction

1. Trace the car cutting pattern on the 2×4, and cut out (Fig. 3-1). Sand smooth (Fig. 3-2).
2. Drill two ½- or 1-inch diameter holes through the car body for windows.
3. Using a hole saw attached to your electric drill, cut out four 1½-inch diameter wheels from the ½-inch scrap. Screw them to the car with the panhead screws.

VAN

Materials

7 inches of 2×4 lumber
scrap of ½-inch-thick wood, large enough to cut out four 1½-inch diameter

Fig. 3-2. This bug car has been sanded properly.

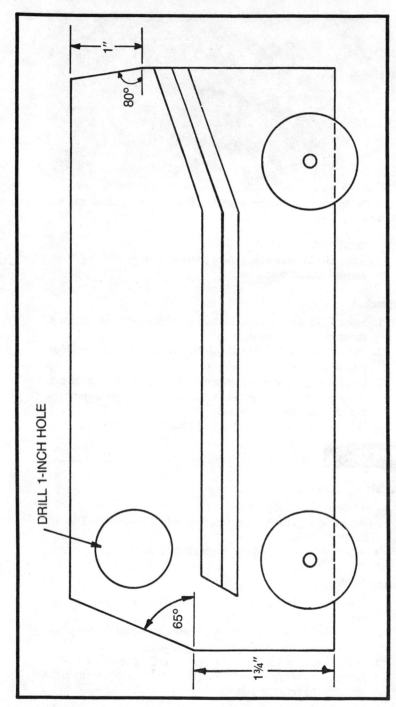

DRILL 1-INCH HOLE

1"

80°

65°

1¾"

Fig. 3-3. Cut the front and rear angles as shown.

47

Fig. 3-4. The finished van may have either a ½-inch or 1-inch diameter hole drilled for the window.

circles
4 No. 10×1¼-inch self-tapping panhead screws
narrow colored tape

Construction

1. Saw a 7-inch-long piece of 2×4. Cut the front and rear angles as shown in Fig. 3-3. Sand smooth.
2. Drill a ½- or 1-inch diameter hole through the van for the window (Fig. 3-4).
3. Using a hole saw attached to an electric drill, cut out four 1½-inch diameter wheels from the ½-inch thick wood. Screw them to the van with the panhead screws.
4. Decorate the van with stripes cut from colored tape.

SCHOOL BUS

Materials

1 foot of 2×4 lumber
scrap of ½-inch thick wood, large enough to cut out four 1½-inch diameter circles
4 No. 10×1¼-inch self-tapping panhead screws

Construction

1. Trace the cutting pattern for the school bus on the 2×4, and saw out (Fig. 3-5). Sand smooth.
2. Drill five ½-inch or 1-inch diameter holes, depending on the power of your drill, through the bus for windows (Fig. 3-6).
3. Using a hole saw attached to an electric drill, cut out four 1½-inch diameter wheels from the ½-inch thick wood. Screw them to the bus with the panhead screws.

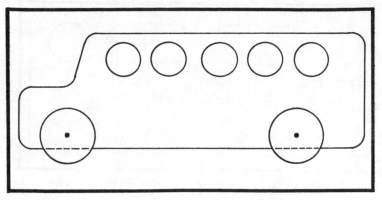

Fig. 3-5. Draw this school bus cutting pattern on a 2 by 4 board.

CITY BUS

Materials

8 inches of 2×4 lumber
scrap of ½-inch thick wood large enough to cut out four 1½-inch diameter circles
4 No. 10×1¼-inch self-tapping panhead screws

Construction

1. Round off all four corners of the 2×4 so that the shape resembles that shown in Fig. 3-7. Sand smooth.
2. Drill seven ¾-inch diameter holes through the 2×4 for windows. To cut the larger windows, drill a hole at either end of the window outline, and then saw out the remainder of the window.
3. Using a hole saw attached to an electric drill, cut out four 1½-inch diameter wheels from the ½-inch thick wood. Screw them to the bus with the panhead screws.

Fig. 3-6. Five ½-inch or 1-inch holes are drilled through the bus for windows.

49

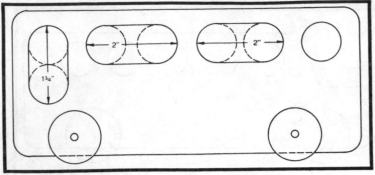

Fig. 3-7. Be sure that the corners of the 2 by 4 look like this illustration.

BUS WITH PEG PEOPLE

Materials

8-inches of 2×4 lumber
2 feet of ⅞-inch diameter dowel
scrap of ½-inch-thick wood large enough to cut
four 1½-inch diameter circles
4 No. 10×1¼-inch self-tapping panhead screws
screw eye and cord

Construction

1. Round the corners of the 2×4 (Fig. 3-8). Sand smooth.
2. Using Fig. 3-8 as a guide, mark the position of the nine peg holes on the 2×4. With a 1-inch diameter spade bit or a Forstner bit, drill nine ½-inch-deep holes in the 2×4.
3. Cut the ⅞-inch diameter dowel into nine 2-inch lengths. Smooth the cut edges. Insert these peg "people" into the nine holes drilled in the 2 × 4 (Fig. 3-9).
4. Using a hole saw attached to an electric drill, cut out four 1½-inch diameter wheels from the ½-inch thick wood. Screw them to the 2×4 with the panhead screws.
5. Attach the screw eye and cord to the front of the bus.

TWO 2 ×2 RACING CARS

2×2 lumber is an ideal size for cutting out all kinds of fancy racing cars. We've given you instructions for two possibilities, which we hope will inspire your own design ideas.

RACER

Materials

7-inches of 2×2 lumber
scrap of 1-inch pine large enough to cut out four
1½-inch diameter circles
4 No. 10×1½-inch shelf-tapping panhead screws

50

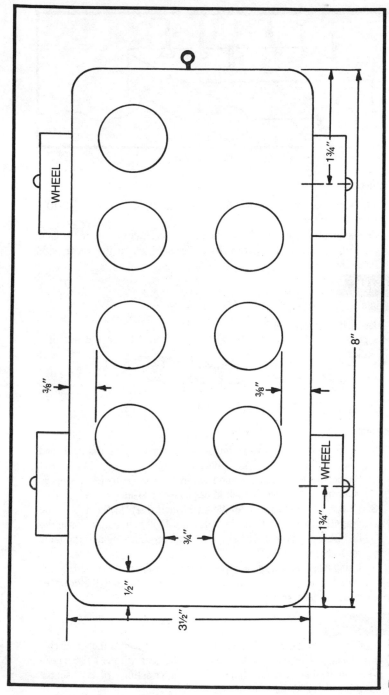

Fig. 3-8. Use this diagram when indicating the position of the nine peg holes on the 2 by 4.

51

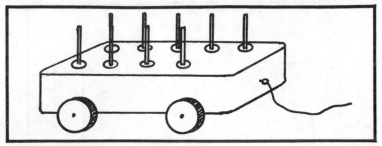

Fig. 3-9. The peg men are placed into the nine holes.

Construction

1. Trace the racer cutting pattern on the 2×2 and cut out (Fig. 3-10). Sand smooth.
2. Using a hole saw attached to an electric drill, cut out four 1½-inch diameter circles from the pine. Screw them to the racer with panhead screws.

DRAGSTER

Materials

8½-inch long piece of 2×2
scrap of 1-inch pine large enough to cut out four 1½-inch diameter circles
scrap of ½-inch-thick wood approximately 1½- × 1¾ inches
4 No. 10×1½-inch self-tapping panhead screws
glue
1½ inches of ¼-inch diameter dowel

Construction

1. Trace the cutting pattern for the dragster body on the 2×2, and saw out (Fig. 3-11). Sand smooth.
2. Shape the ½-inch-thick wood scrap with a file to form a fin as illustrated. Cut two ¾-inch-long pieces of ¼-inch dowel.
3. Drill two ¼-inch diameter holes ¼ inch deep in the top of the dragster, ⅜ inch in from the rear end. Drill matching holes in the fin. Glue the ¼-inch dowel pegs between the body and the fin in these holes.
4. Using a hole saw attached to an electric drill, cut out four 1½-inch diameter wheels from the 1-inch pine. Screw them to the dragster with panhead screws.

1 × 2 CARS

These vehicles are recollections of some we saw at a local church's Christmas bazaar. The six cars—a sedan, a police car, a taxi, a fire chief's car, a station wagon, and an ambulance—are variations of two simple designs, the sedan and the station wagon.

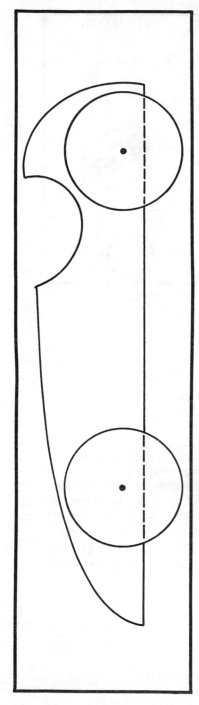

Fig. 3-10. This racing car pattern is outlined on a 2 by 2.

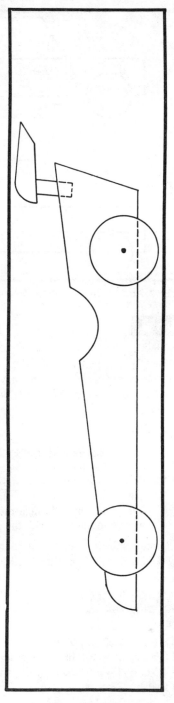

Fig. 3-11. The dragster body cutting pattern is also traced on a 2 by 2.

53

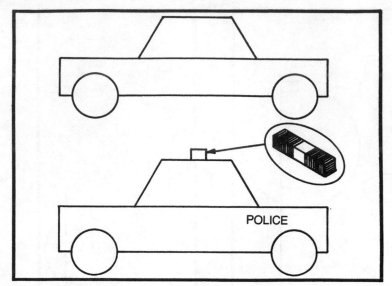

Fig. 3-12. Angle each long corner on the car body and top.

Materials

1 foot of 1×2 pine
3 inches of ¾-inch diameter dowel
4 No. 6×1¼-inch self tapping panhead screws
glue

Construction

1. Cut a 5-inch-long piece of 1×2 for the car body, and a second piece of 1×2 for the top. Angle each long corner (Fig. 3-12).
2. Glue the top to the body, and clamp together until the glue is dry.
3. Cut the ¾-inch dowel into four ½-inch-thick slices for wheels. Drill a 9/64-inch hole through the center of each wheel. Screw the wheels to the base with the panhead screws.

Modifications: Tack a wood scrap to the roof top to resemble a light. Print POLICE, TAXI, or FIRE CHIEF in block letters on either side of the car.

STATION WAGON

Materials

8½ inches of 1×2 pine
3 inches of ¾-inch diameter dowel
4 No. 6×1¼-inch self tapping panhead screws
glue

Construction

1. Cut a 5-inch-long piece of 1×2 pine for the body. Angle the rear end (Fig. 3-13).
2. Cut a second piece of 1×2, approximately 3½ inches long, with each 1½-inch corner angled like the diagram.
3. Glue the smaller piece to the larger so that it is flush with one end. Clamp the two together until the glue is dry.
4. Cut the ¾-inch dowel into four ½-inch-thick slices for wheels. Drill a 9/64-inch hole through the center of each wheel. Screw the wheels to the base with panhead screws.

Ambulance modification: Tack on a small scrap of dowel for roof light. Decorate with a red cross and the word AMBULANCE.

SEMI-TRAILER TRUCK CAB

Instructions for three hook-ups—a flatbed, a log carrier, and a semi—are given on the following pages. Use scraps from any kind of 2×4 lumber to build this cab. The one in Fig. 3-14 was made from end pieces of redwood left over from a patio deck project.

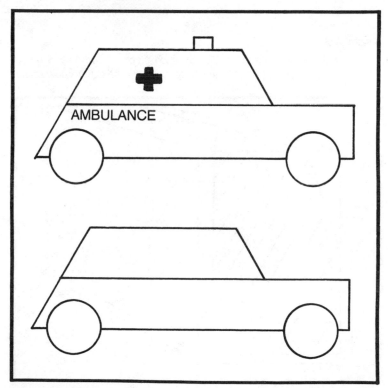

Fig. 3-13. The station wagon's rear end must be angled as shown.

Fig. 3-14. This semi-trailer truck cab was built with end pieces of redwood.

Materials

    5 inches of 2×4 lumber
    9 inches of ¼-inch diameter dowel
    6 inches of 1- × 4-inch pine
    6 inches of ½- × 4-inch pine
    4 No. 10×1¼-inch self-tapping panhead screws
    8d finishing nails
    glue

Construction

1. Saw the 2×4 into two 2½×3½-inch pieces. From one of these pieces, slice off one 3½-inch edge to form the cab window shape

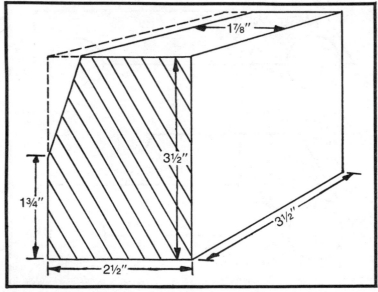

Fig. 3-15. The diagram shows how to form the cab window shape.

(Fig. 3-15). Sand any rough areas smooth. Glue the two pieces together as illustrated, and clamp until dry.

2. Drill two ¼-inch diameter holes ½ inch deep in the 1- × 4-inch pine. Refer to Fig. 3-16.

3. Nail the 1- × 4-inch piece to the 2×4 assembly so that the 2×4 is in front of the ¼-inch holes and flush with one end of the 1- × 4-inch piece.

4. From the ½-inch-thick pine cut four 1½-inch diameter wheels with a hole saw attached to an electric drill. Also saw off a ½- × ½- × 3½-inch strip.

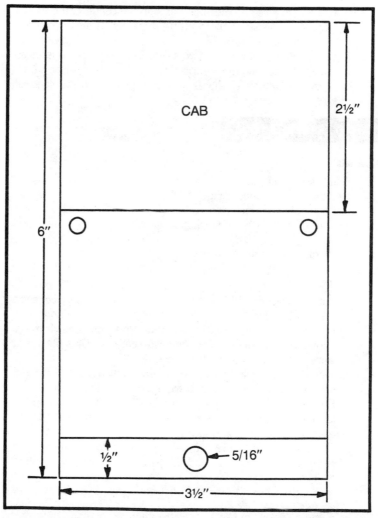

Fig. 3-16. Place the two holes in the 1 by 4-inch pine as illustrated.

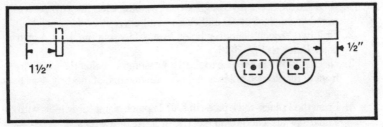

Fig. 3-17. Fasten the 3¼-inch piece to the end opposite the dowel.

5. Drill a 5/16-inch diameter hole through the center of the ½-inch strip. Glue this strip flush with the back end of the 1- × 4-inch piece. Clamp until dry.
6. Cut the ¼-inch dowel into two 4½-inch-long pieces. Glue these "smokestacks" into the predrilled holes of the 1- × 4-inch piece.
7. Screw the wheels to the 1- × 4-inch piece with the panhead screws.

FLATBED TRAILER TRUCK

Materials

Semi-trailer truck cab
16 inches of 1- × 4-inch pine
6 inches of ½- × 4-inch pine
four No. 10×1¼-inch self tapping panhead screws
6d finishing nails
1 inch of ¼-inch diameter dowel

Construction

1. Cut two pieces from the 1- × 4-inch pine, a 12-inch-long piece and a 3¼-inch-long piece.
2. Drill a ½-inch-deep ¼-inch diameter hole in the 12-inch piece, 1½-inches in from one short end and centered. Glue the 1-inch piece of ¼-inch dowel in this hole (Fig. 3-17).
3. Glue and nail the 3¼-inch piece to the 12-inch piece at the end opposite the dowel, ½ inch in from the edge (Fig. 3-18).
4. From the ½-inch-thick pine saw out four 1½-inch diameter wheels and two ½- × ½- × 3½-inch strips. Use a hole saw attached to an electric drill to saw out the wheels.
5. Glue and nail the two ½-inch strips to the bottom of the 3¼-inch piece so that they are 1¼ inches apart and ½ inch in from either end.
6. Screw the wheels to the ½-inch wood strips with the panhead screws.
7. Set the dowel peg into the 5/16-inch hole in the truck cab.

Fig. 3-18. Proper gluing and nailing produces a nice flatbed trailer truck.

LOG TRUCK

A few simple additions to the flatbed trailer produces a log hauling truck (Fig. 3-19). If you don't glue the dowels in place, your children can then change the log truck into the flatbed and vice versa when they wish.

Materials

Flatbed trailer truck
18 inches of ¼-inch diameter dowel
logs: 3 pieces of 1¼-inch diameter pole 12 inches long, or tree branches cut approximately to size
glue

Construction

1. Drill six ½-inch-deep ¼-inch diameter holes in the top of the flatbed platform (Fig. 3-20).

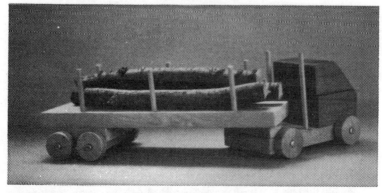

Fig. 3-19. Just a few easy additions to the flatbed trailer results in a beautiful log truck.

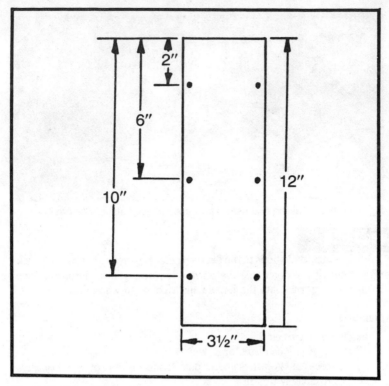

Fig. 3-20. This diagram illustrates where to drill the six holes in the flatbed platform's top.

2. Cut the ¼-inch dowel into six 2½-inch-long pieces. Glue one piece into each hole.
3. Pile "logs" on the truck (Fig. 3-21).

SEMI-TRAILER TRUCK

Four straight cuts across a 1×4 board are all the sawing you'll have to do to complete this project (Fig. 3-22).

Materials

flatbed trailer truck assembly
3½ feet of 1×4 pine
8d finishing nails

Construction

1. Build the flatbed trailer truck through step 2.
2. Cut the pine into the following pieces: a 2-inch-long end piece, two 12-inch-long side pieces, and one 12-inch-long roof piece.

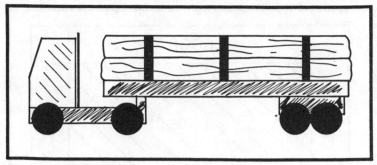

Fig. 3-21. Place the logs on the truck in this manner.

3. Nail the roof piece between the two side pieces. Nail the end piece in place so that it is surrounded by the sides and roof. Nail the sides to the flatbed platform. Refer to Figs. 3-23 and 3-24.

4. Continue with steps 3–7 of the flatbed trailer truck instructions.

MILK TRUCK

The home-delivery milk truck seems to be going the way of the horse and buggy, but a few are still around. This toy version should have no competition in your child's truck fleet (Fig. 3-25). There may be commercially made versions around, but we've yet to find one.

Materials

2 feet of ½- ×12-inch pine
6d finishing nails
4 No. 10×1¼-inch self-tapping panhead screws
paint

Fig. 3-22. The semi-trailer truck was made with four pieces which were cut across a 1 by 4-inch board.

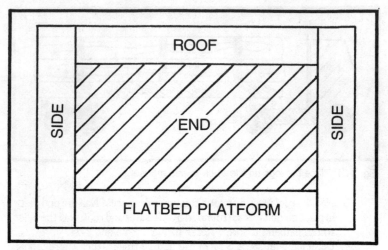

Fig. 3-23. The illustration shows how to nail the various pieces together.

Construction

1. Saw out the following pieces from the pine:
   roof—one rectangle 4½ × 5 inches, with one 4½-inch edge beveled 45°
   sides—two pieces 4×5½ inches (use Fig. 3-26)
   hood—one rectangle 1½× 4-inches
   front—one rectangle 2× 4 inches
   base—one rectangle 4½ × 6½ inches
2. Saw out four 1½-inch diameter wheels from the pine with a hole saw attached to an electric drill.
3. Nail the hood and front to the sides as illustrated (Fig. 3-27).

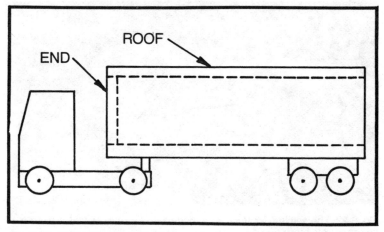

Fig. 3-24. Nail the truck's end piece as shown.

Fig. 3-25. This milk truck is ready for your child to make deliveries.

4. Nail the roof to the sides so that it is flush with the rear, and overhangs each side by ¼ inch.
5. Nail the truck body to the base so that the base extends ¼ inch around the body of the truck.
6. Sand any sharp edges, and then paint.
7. Screw the wheels to the base with the panhead screws (Fig. 3-28).

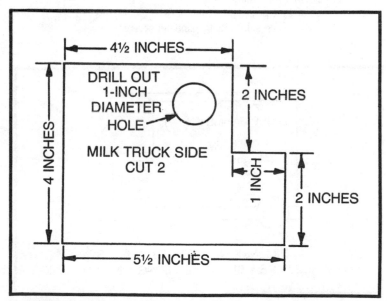

Fig. 3-26. Use this cutting pattern for the milk truck's sides.

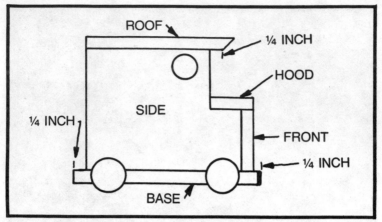

Fig. 3-27. This drawing shows the proper way to fasten the truck's hood and front to the sides.

BASIC TRUCK

This truck is the base on which you can build the more elaborate vehicles on the following pages—the moving van, dump truck, and pickup (Fig. 3-29).

Materials

3½ inches of 2×4 lumber
18 inches of 1×4 pine
6 No. 10×1½-inch self-tapping panhead screws
glue

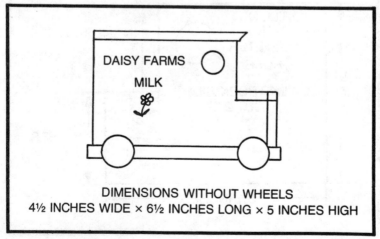

Fig. 3-28. Use panhead screws to attach the truck's wheels to its base.

Fig. 3-29. A moving van, dump truck and pickup can be built using this truck as a base.

Construction

1. Sand the cut ends of the 2×4 smooth.
2. From the 1×4 pine, saw off a 9-inch-long piece. Glue the 2×4 to the 9-inch platform, ¼-inch in from one end.
3. Cut a second piece from the 1×4 pine, 2 inches long with one edge beveled to form a windshield. Glue this piece to the top of the 2×4 as shown in Fig. 3-30.
4. Using a hole saw attached to an electric drill, cut out six 1½-inch diameter wheels from the 1×4 pine. Attach them to the truck with panhead screws.

MOVING VAN

Materials

Basic truck
2 feet of ½- × 4-inch pine
6d finishing nails
glue

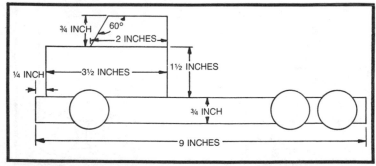

Fig. 3-30. Glue the 2-inch pine piece to the top of the 2 by 4.

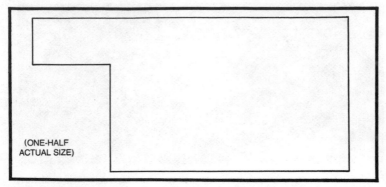

Fig. 3-31. Trace the moving van side cutting pattern on a ½-inch thick pine board.

Construction

1. From the ½-inch-thick pine cut two van sides using the cutting pattern provided (Fig. 3-31), one 1- × 3½-inch rectangle for the end, and one 2½- × 6-inch rectangle for the top.
2. Assemble the van by nailing the sides to the top, and the end to the top and sides (Fig. 3-32).
3. Glue and nail the van to the basic truck platform.

DUMP TRUCK

Materials

Basic truck
2 feet of ½- × 4-inch clear pine
one ¾- × 2-inch butt hinge with screws
6d finishing nails
glue

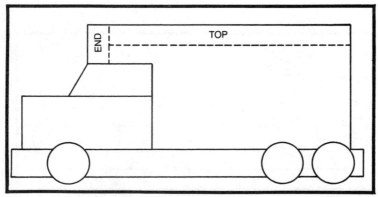

Fig. 3-32. This diagram illustrates proper nailing of the van's pieces.

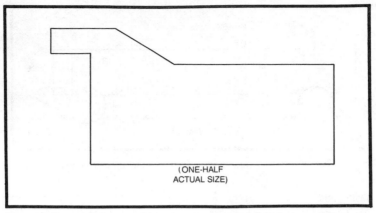

(ONE-HALF
ACTUAL SIZE)

Fig. 3-33. Copy the dumper sides pattern on a ½-inch thick pine and then saw carefully.

Construction

1. From the ½-inch thick pine, cut out two dumper sides using the cutting pattern provided, one 3½- × 5-inch rectangle for the dumper base, and one 2⅜- × 3½-inch rectangle for the dumper end (Fig. 3-33). Sand the rough edges.
2. Build the dumper by nailing the sides to the end, and the base to the sides and end (Fig. 3-34).
3. Cut mortises for the butt hinge in the dumper base and in the platform of the basic truck. Attach hinge.

PICKUP TRUCK

Materials

Basic truck
10 feet of 1×2 pine
8d finishing nails
glue

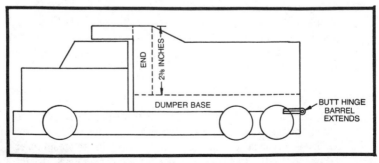

Fig. 3-34. Nail the dumper's pieces together as shown.

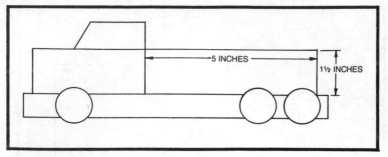

Fig. 3-35. Two 1½ by 5-inch rectangles form the pickup truck's sides.

Construction

1. Cut two 1½- × 5-inch rectangles from the pine to form the sides of the pickup truck (Fig. 3-35). Sand the rough edges.
2. Glue and nail one rectangle to either side of the platform of the basic truck (Fig. 3-36).

STEAM ROLLER

The steam roller is a favorite toy with kids. They are particularly impressed with the rollers and smokestack. Children often use this toy when they are pretending to make a road or highway. For example, the steam roller is pushed across the road material (usually dirt) to level or flatten it.

You will have to drill several holes when building the steam roller. The location of holes in wood should be marked by two crossing lines. If there could be confusion with other crossing lines, put a small freehand pencil ring around the place. It is good policy to drill holes after wood has been marked out and before other work is done to it.

Materials

5½ inches of 2×2
3½ inches of 1½-inch diameter pole
¼-inch thick wood scrap
7 inches of ½- × 4-inch pine
1 foot of ¼-inch diameter dowel
2 No. 12×1¼-inch roundhead screws
glue
brads

Construction

1. Saw out the body of the steam roller from the 2×2, using the cutting pattern Fig. 3-37. Sand smooth.
2. Drill seven ¼-inch diameter holes ½ inch deep in the steam roller body: four for the roof supports, one for the smokestack, two for the roller holders (Fig. 3-38).

Fig. 3-36. The pickup truck includes one rectangle glued and nailed to either side of the basic truck's platform.

3. Cut four 1½-inch long pieces of ¼-inch dowel, and glue them into the roof support holes. Cut one 1¼-inch-long piece of ¼-inch dowel, and glue it in the smokestack hole. Cut two 1¾-inch-long pieces of ¼-inch dowel, and glue them in the roller holder holes.
4. From the ¼-inch-thick wood, cut a 1¾- × 2¼-inch roof piece. Brad this roof piece to the four roof support dowels.
5. Cut two 3-inch diameter circles to be used as wheels from the ½-inch thick pine. Sand smooth. Drill a ¼-inch diameter hole through the center of each wheel. Screw the wheels to the body with the roundhead screws.
6. Insert a 3½-inch-long piece of 1½-inch diameter pole between the body and the roller holders. The roller is not attached to the body (Fig. 3-39).

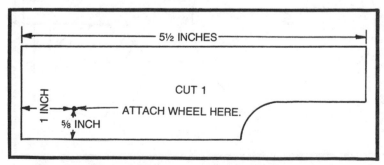

Fig. 3-37. Trace the steam roller body pattern on a 2 by 2 carefully.

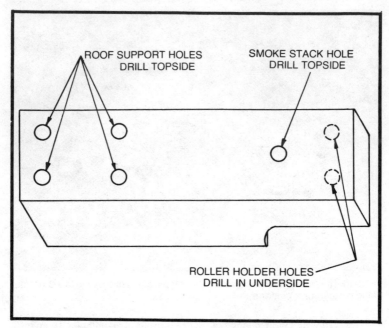

Fig. 3-38. This illustration shows proper placement of roof support, smokestack and roller holders holes.

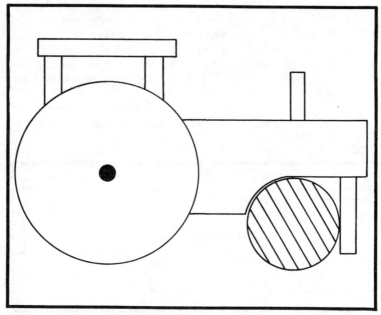

Fig. 3-39. Do not fasten the roller to the body or frame.

Fig. 3-40. This completed tractor is ready for work.

TRACTOR

No farm would be complete without a tractor. This vehicle is used by farmers to pull farm machinery and haul loads. Your kids will enjoy pushing it around (Fig. 3-40).

Materials

scrap of 2×2 at least 4 inches long
scrap of ½×6 inches at least 4 inches long
1⅜ inch of ⅜-inch diameter dowel
scrap of ¼ inch thick wood
four No. 8×1¼ inch roundhead screws
glue

Construction

1. Using Fig. 3-41, saw out one engine from the 2×2. Round off one edge as shown.
2. Cut a 1½×4½ inch base from the ½ inch thick wood. Drill a ⅜ inch diameter, ¼ inch deep blind hole in the midline of the base, ¼ inch from one end. Glue the dowel piece in this hole.
3. Saw off a ½ inch slice of 2×2 and glue it to the underside of the base to serve as the front wheel axle.
4. Glue the base to the tractor engine as shown in Fig. 3-42.
5. From the ½-inch thick wood, cut two 2½ inch diameter wheels and two ¾-inch diameter wheels. Drill six ½-inch diameter holes in the larger wheels as illustrated.
6. Screw the 2½ inch wheels to either side of the base 1 inch from the back end. Screw the ¾ inch wheels to either side of the front axle.

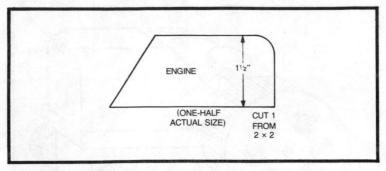

Fig. 3-41. The tractor engine cutting pattern. Cut one pattern from a 2 by 2.

7. Cut out a 1 inch circle from ¼ inch thick wood for the seat. Drill a ⅜ inch diameter, ⅛ inch deep blind hole on the underside of the center of the seat. Glue the seat to the dowel.

FIRE ENGINE

Most little boys would like to be firemen when they grow up. They view firefighters as brave, adventurous souls who enjoy helping and rescuing people. This fire engine toy will fascinate the future flame extinguisher. The ladder and wheels make it seem realistic.

Materials

6 feet of ½- × 6-inch pine
2 feet of ¼-inch diameter dowel
13 inches of ⅛-inch diameter dowel
1½-inch piece of 1-inch diameter dowel
6 No. 10×1¼-inch self-tapping panhead screws
6d finishing nails
glue

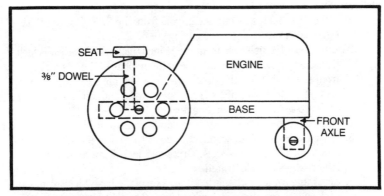

Fig. 3-42. Fasten the tractor parts together as the diagram illustrates.

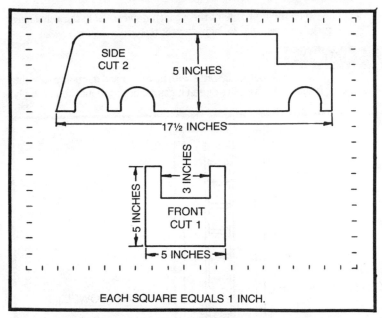

Fig. 3-43. Trace the fire engine sides and front patterns on ½-inch thick wood.

Construction

1. Saw out the following pieces from the ½-inch-thick pine:
   truck base—one rectangle 4 × 17½ inches
   sides—two pieces 5 × 17½ inches (use Fig. 3-43)
   front—one piece 5 × 5 inches (use Fig. 3-43)
   roof—one square 5 × 5 inches with one edge beveled 45°
   ladder base—one square 2×2
   wheels—six 2-inch diameter circles.
2. Using Fig. 3-44 as a guide, glue and nail the front and sides to the truck base, and the roof to the sides and front.
3. Drill a 1-inch diameter hole through the center of the ladder base. Glue the ladder base to the truck base, 5½ inches from the front end.
4. Drill a ⅛-inch diameter hole through the side of the 1-inch diameter dowel, ½ inch from one end. Glue this dowel into the ladder base hole so that the ⅛-inch hole is exposed.
5. Attach the six wheels to the truck base with panhead screws.
6. To build the ladder, first cut two 10½-inch lengths of ¼-inch diameter dowel for the ladder sides. Starting ½ inch from one end, drill eight ⅛-inch diameter holes through the sides of each ¼-inch dowel, spacing the holes 1 inch apart. Cut the ⅛-inch dowel into eight 1½-inch long ladder rungs. Insert one rung through the 1-inch dowel glued to the ladder base, and then glue this same rung

73

between the first hole of the ¼-inch dowels. Glue the remaining rungs between the ¼-inch dowels to form a ladder.

The gas station is another favorite with boys. Air and gas pumps are the interesting features. We've never seen a gas station without them. Simply

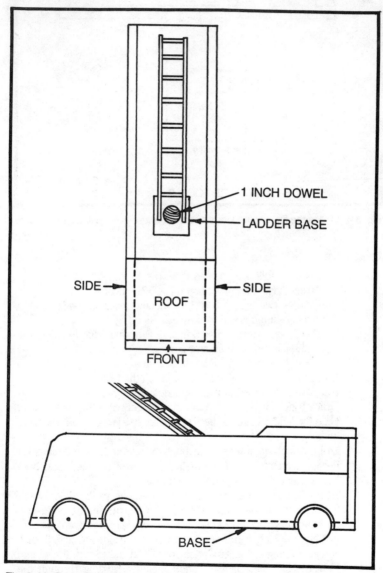

Fig. 3-44. Connect the front, sides and roof to the base as shown.

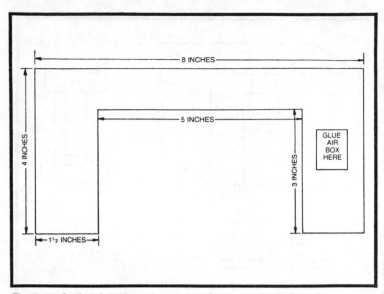

Fig. 3-45. Outline the gas station garage front on ½-inch pine.

cut the pump pieces out of the wood and glue them to the front and pump base. You might even paint the name of the station's gas in small letters on the pump to let your son's "customers" know what fuel is available.

Materials

    2½ feet of ½- × 10-inch pine
    1 feet of 1×1 wood strip
    8 inches of ¼-inch diameter dowel
    6d finishing nails
    glue
    paint

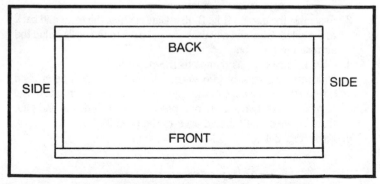

Fig. 3-46. Fasten the garage's front, sides and back as shown.

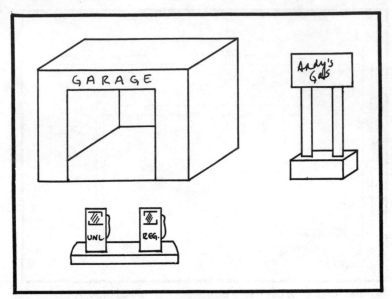

Fig. 3-47. Andy's garage is "open for business."

Construction

1. From the ½-inch wood cut out the following pieces:
   sides—two rectangles, 4 × 5 inches
   back—one rectangle, 4 × 8 inches
   front—one piece, 4 × 8 inches (use Fig. 3-45)
   roof and base—two rectangles, 6 × 8 inches
   sign top—one rectangle, 2 × 3 inches
   air pump—one rectangle, ¾ × 1 inches
2. Cut the 1×1 into:
   gas pumps—two 2½-inch-long pieces
   gas pump base—one 6-inch-long piece
   sign base—one 3-inch-long piece.
3. Assemble the garage (Fig. 3-45). Glue and nail the front and back to the sides. Glue and nail the roof and base to the walls. Glue the air pump to the front.
4. Glue and nail the gas pumps to the pump base.
5. Drill matching sets of two ¼-inch diameter, ½-inch-deep blind holes in the 3-inch edge of the sign top and in the 1-inch side of the sign base. Cut two 4-inch-long pieces of ¼-inch dowel and glue them between the top and base in the predrilled holes.
6. Paint (Fig. 3-47).

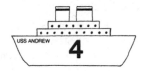

Trains, Planes, Boats, and Other Vehicles

This chapter features more "transportation" toys that your young son, or possibly daughter, will like. You might build a tot train or the popular circus train in which the kids can place their animals. Other items of interest in this chapter include two planes, a helicopter, an aircraft carrier, a tank, a covered wagon and a whole fleet of boats and ships. You'll need plenty of glue and finishing nails to construct these toys.

TOT'S TRAIN

If you would like to make a train in which your toddlers can haul their stuffed animals around, double all the dimensions given in the instructions. For example, instead of cutting a 2½- × 6-inch base, cut a 5- × 12-inch base (Fig. 4-1). You'll have to make a trip to a fabric store to buy the toggle buttons and closings.

Materials

5 feet of ½- × 6-inch pine
8 inches of ¼-inch diameter dowel
2¼ inch of ¾-inch diameter dowel
16 No. 10×1¼-inch self-tapping panhead screws
four toggle buttons and closings
screw eye and cord
6d finishing nails
glue
staples
paint

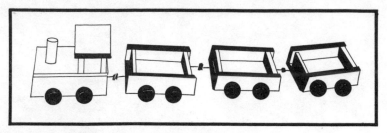

Fig. 4-1. Use a 5 by 2-inch base for "passenger" train cars.

Construction

1. Cut out the listed pieces from the ½-inch-thick pine. Use a hole saw attached to an electric drill to cut out the wheels.

    base—4 rectangles, 2½ × 6 inches
    side—8 rectangles, 2 × 6 inches
    end—8 rectangles, 1½ × 2½ inches
    engine cab roof—1 rectangle, 2½ × 3½ inches
    engine hood—1 rectangle, 3½ × 6 inches
    axles—8 strips, 1 × 3¾ inches
    wheels—16 1½-inch diameter circles.

2. Assemble four boxcars. Use Figs. 4-2 and 4-3 as guides while working. First, glue and nail two axles to the underside of the base of each car. Next, glue and nail the ends to the bases. Then, glue and nail the sides to the bases and ends. Attach the wheels to the axles with the panhead screws.

3. Use one of the assembled boxcars as the base for building the engine (Fig. 4-4). In the top of the engine hood piece, drill one ¾-inch diameter blind hole ¼ inch deep for the smokestack, and

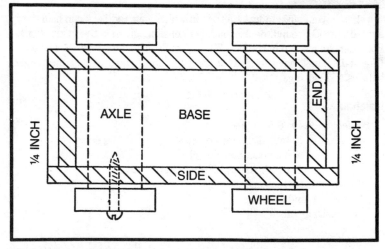

Fig. 4-2. Fasten the boxcars' axles and ends as shown.

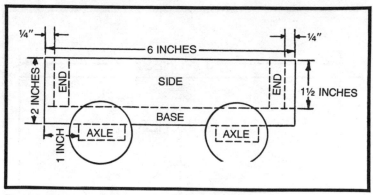

Fig. 4-3. Fasten the wheels to the axles with reliable panhead screws.

four ¼-inch diameter blind holes ¼ inch deep for the cab roof supports. Refer to Fig. 4-5.

4. Nail the engine hood to the top of the boxcar so that the predrilled holes are on top.

5. Glue a 2¼-inch-long piece of ¾-inch dowel in the smokestack hole, and the four 1¾-inch-long pieces of ¼-inch dowel in the roof support holes.

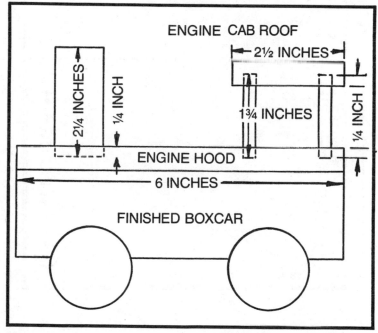

Fig. 4-4. A completed boxcar serves as the engine's base.

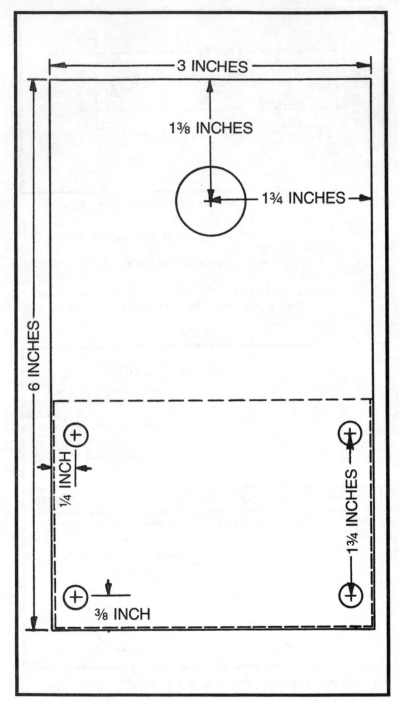

Fig. 4-5. This engine hood drilling diagram shows proper placement of blind holes.

6. Drill four ¼-inch diameter, ¼-inch deep blind holes in the engine cab roof so that they match up with the roof support dowels in the engine hood. Glue the roof supports in these holes.
7. Staple the toggle buttons and closings to the underside of the bases of the engine and boxcars.
8. Attach a screw eye and cord to the front of the engine.

CIRCUS TRAIN

The two wild animal cage cars make this train a special one for small children (Fig. 4-6). If you feel extra ambitious, saw out a few wild animal shapes from the ½-inch pine to put in the cages. This train looks best painted in bright colors.

Materials

3 feet of ½- × 8-inch clear pine
scrap of ¼-inch-thick plywood, at least 6 × 12 inches
3½ inches of 1½-inch diameter pole
2¼ inches of ¾-inch diameter dowel
½-inch piece of ½-inch diameter dowel
8 feet of ⅛-inch diameter dowel
18 No. 10×1¼-inch self-tapping panhead screws
6d finishing nails
glue
4 screw eyes and hooks

Construction

1. Cut out the listed pieces from the ½-inch pine. Use a hole saw attached to an electric drill to cut out the wheels.

Fig. 4-6. These circus train cage cars can carry animals like tigers and elephants, much to the kids' delight.

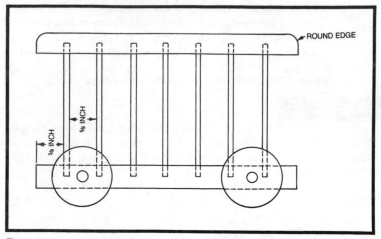

Fig. 4-7. Round off the top edges of the cage car roof as shown.

> base—4 rectangles, 3 × 6 inches
> engine cab sides—3 rectangles, 2 × 2½ inches
> engine sides—2 rectangles, 1×2 with one corner rounded
> cab roof—1 rectangle, 2½ × 3 inches
> boxcar sides—2 rectangles, 1 × 6 inches
> boxcar ends—2 rectangles, 1×2
> wheels—18 1½ inch diameter circles.

2. Cut out four wild animal cage roofs from the ¼-inch-thick wood, each 3 × 6 inches. Round off the top edges around the perimeter of two roof pieces (Fig. 4-7).

3. Drill 1-inch diameter window holes in the three engine cab sides (Fig. 4-8).

4. Sand the pieces smooth. Prime and paint all the pieces, including the dowels.

Engine Assembly: Make one.

5. Drill a ½-inch diameter blind hole, ¼ inch deep, centered in one end of the 3½-inch length of 1½-inch pole. Cut a ½-inch piece of ½-inch dowel, and glue it in this hole (Fig. 4-9).

6. On the top side of the 1½-inch pole, drill two ¼-inch deep, ¾-inch diameter blind holes. Cut two pieces of ¾-inch diameter dowel—a 1½-inch piece and a ¾-inch piece. Glue the 1½-inch-long piece in the first hole, and the ¾-inch-long piece in the second hole.

7. Glue and nail the three engine cab sides to the base. Center the 1½-inch diameter pole in front of the cab sides and glue and nail it to the base. Glue and nail the engine side panels to either side of the pole, ¼ inch in from the edge of the base, and flush with the front of the cab. Attach the cab roof so that it overhangs the front and back of the cab by ¼ inch.

8. Attach six wheels to the engine base with panhead screws.

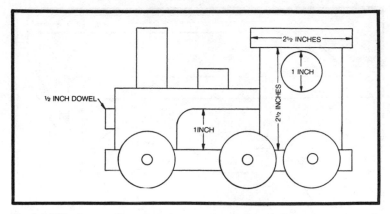

Fig. 4-8. This diagram illustrates where to place window holes in the engine cab sides.

Wild Animal Cage Car Assembly: Make two.

9. Tape one wild animal cage roof that has not had its edges rounded to a base piece so that the two match up exactly. Drill seven ⅛-inch diameter holes on either side of the roof and base, 14 holes in all, drilling through the roof piece and ¼ inch deep into the base. Untape.

10. Glue a roof piece with rounded edges to the top of the predrilled roof piece, so that the rounded edges are on top. Clamp together until dry.

11. Cut the ⅛-inch diameter dowel into 28 3⅛-inch-long pieces. Glue 14 pieces between the base and roof in the predrilled holes.

12. Attach four wheels to each cage car base with panhead screws.

Boxcar Assembly

13. Glue and nail the boxcar sides and ends to the base (Fig. 4-10).

14. Attach four wheels with panhead screws.

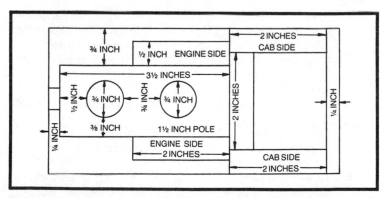

Fig. 4-9. Refer to this drawing for proper circus train engine assembly.

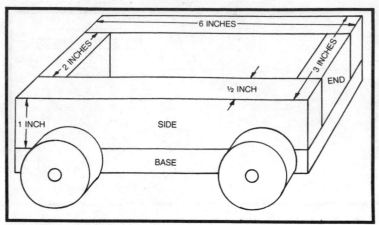

Fig. 4-10. Fasten the boxcar pieces as shown.

Finishing

15. Varnish the train.
16. Attach screw eyes and screw hooks to the front and rear of the engine and cars.

SMILING PLANE

This cute, grinning plane would make Orville and Wilbur Wright proud.

Materials

1 foot of 1×6 clear pine
2 feet of ½- × 4-inch clear pine
2 feet of ¼-inch diameter dowel
6d finishing nails
1 No. 6×1-inch roundhead screw
glue
paint

Construction

1. Enlarge the fuselage cutting pattern (Fig. 4-11), trace it on the ¾-inch pine, and saw out. Drill a ⅜-inch diameter hole through the fuselage at the point indicated on the pattern. Sand smooth.
2. Cut out the following pieces from the ½-inch pine and sand smooth:
     wing—one rectangle, 3½ × 14¾ inches, with rounded corners
     tail—one rectangle, 2 × 4¼ inches, with rounded corners
     wheels—two 2-inch diameter circles
     propeller—one piece; use cutting pattern.
3. Glue and nail the wing and tail in place.
4. Drill a ¼-inch diameter hole through the center of each wheel. Insert the dowel through the hole in the fuselage and glue the wheels to either end.

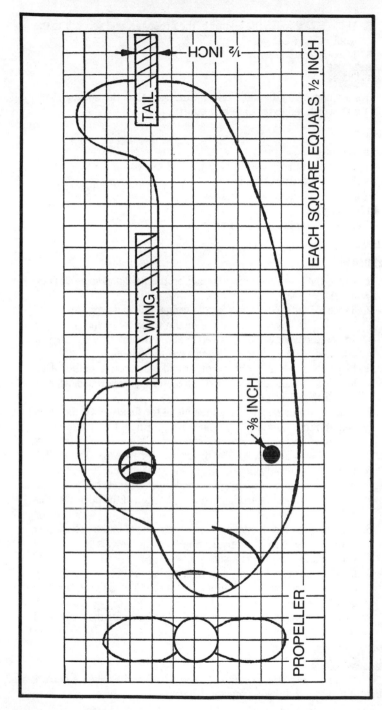

Fig. 4-11. Carefully trace this smiling plane fuselage pattern on ¾-inch pine.

5. Drill a hole through the center of the propeller, and screw it to the front of the fuselage.
6. Decorate as you wish.

BI-PLANE

This toy may be a little more difficult to make than the smiling plane. But it's well worth the extra time and effort.

Materials

6 inches of 2×2
scrap of ¼-inch-thick wood, at least 8 × 8 inches
1 inch of ¼-inch diameter dowel
1¼ inches of ½-inch diameter dowel
4d finishing nails
1 No. 4×1-inch roundhead screw
glue

Construction

1. Trace the fuselage cutting outline on the 2×2 and saw out (Fig. 4-12). Sand smooth.
2. Trace the cutting patterns for the wings, tail, and propeller on the ¼-inch thick wood. Also outline on the wood two 1-inch diameter circles for wheels. Saw out and sand smooth. Use a hole saw attached to an electric drill to cut out the wheels.
3. Place one wing on top of the other and tape them together. Drill four ¼-inch diameter holes through both wings where indicated on the pattern. Untape.
4. Glue the lower wing to the underside of the fuselage. At the exact center of the wing, drill a ¼-inch diameter hole through the wing and extending ¼ inch into the fuselage. Glue a 1⅛-inch piece of ¼-inch dowel in this hole. Nail the wing to the fuselage (Fig. 4-13).
5. Drill one ¼-inch diameter, ¼-inch-deep blind hole ½ inch in the midpoint of a 1¼-inch-long piece of ½-inch diameter dowel. Glue the ¼-inch dowel protruding from the bottom of the plane into this hole.
6. Glue four 2¼-inch long pieces of ¼-inch dowel in the holes in the bottom wing. Glue the upper wing onto the dowels.
7. Glue and nail the tail in place.
8. Drill ½-inch diameter holes through the center of each wheel (Fig. 4-14). Glue the wheels to either end of the ½-inch dowel "landing gear" (step 5).
9. Attach the propeller to the front of the fuselage with the roundhead screw.

HELICOPTER

This popular craft is complete with rotor blades. It makes a perfect addition to your son's already crowded hangar.

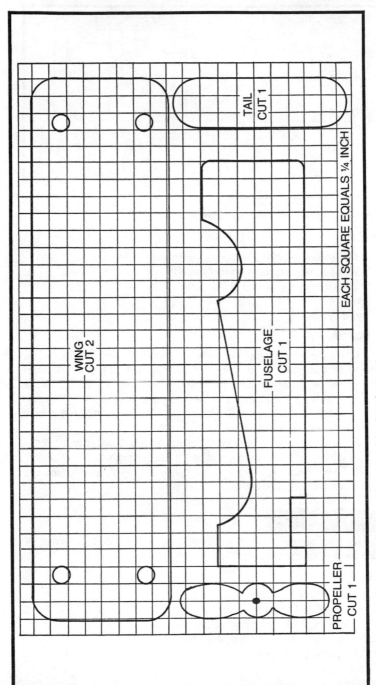

WING
CUT 2

TAIL
CUT 1

FUSELAGE
CUT 1

PROPELLER
CUT 1

EACH SQUARE EQUALS ¼ INCH

Fig. 4-12. Draw the bi-plane fuselage pattern on a 2 by 2 and cut out.

87

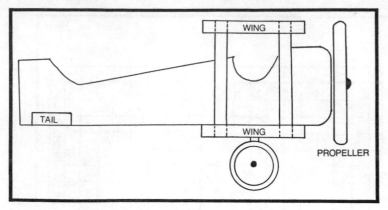

Fig. 4-13. Fasten the wings to the bi-plane as shown.

Materials

2 feet of ½- × 4-inch clear pine
4-inch square scrap of ¼-inch plywood
¼-inch diameter dowel, 1¼ inch long
glue
paint, varnish

Construction

1. Enlarge the cutting patterns for pieces A and B (Fig. 4-15). Transfer them to the ½-inch-thick wood and cut out two A pieces and one B piece. Outline the rotor blade cutting pattern on the ¼-inch-thick wood and cut out one piece (Fig. 4-16).
2. Drill a ¼-inch diameter ½-inch deep blind hole in the top ½-inch edge of piece B as shown in the pattern.
3. Sandwich piece B between the two A pieces, and glue the three pieces together. Clamp until dry. Sand smooth.
4. Glue the dowel in the predrilled hole in the top of piece B. Glue the rotor blades to the top of this dowel.
5. Paint and/or varnish.

AIRCRAFT CARRIER

Buy a set of tiny planes at the dimestore to use with this carrier, or make a few from balsa wood.

Materials

14 inches of 1- × 4-inch pine
scrap of ¼-inch-thick plywood, at least 7 × 13 inches
1¼-inch piece of 1 inch diameter dowel
2½-inch piece of ⅛-inch diameter dowel
4d finishing nails
glue
paint

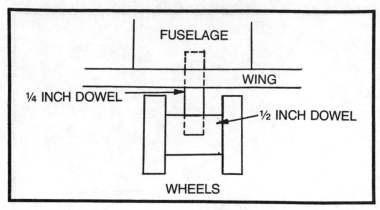

Fig. 4-14. Attach the bi-plane's wheels as illustrated.

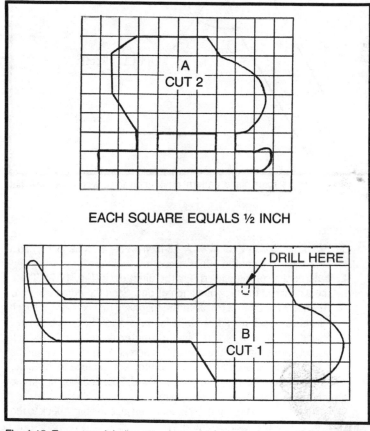

EACH SQUARE EQUALS ½ INCH

Fig. 4-15. Trace two A helicopter pieces and one B piece carefully on ½-Inch thick wood.

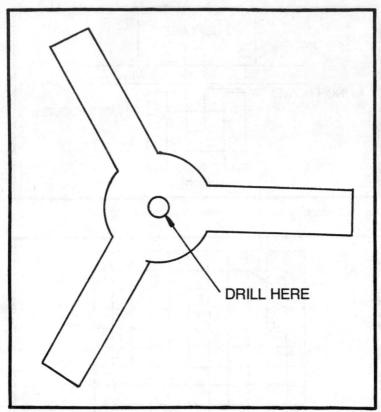

DRILL HERE

Fig. 4-16. Draw this rotor blade pattern on ¼-inch thick wood and saw out carefully.

Construction

1. From the pine saw one 3½- × 12-inch piece, a 1×1 square, and a 2×2 square. Sand the edges smooth.
2. Enlarge the cutting pattern for the flight deck (Fig. 4-17). Trace the pattern on the plywood and cut out. Sand the edges smooth.
3. Assemble the control tower in the following manner: drill a 1-inch diameter ½-inch-deep blind hole in one side of the 2-inch square. Round off one end of the 1-inch diameter dowel. Drill a ⅛-inch diameter hole through the side of this dowel, ¼ inch down from the rounded end. Glue the ⅛-inch diameter dowel piece in this hole, and then glue the 1-inch diameter dowel, rounded side up, in the predrilled hole of the 2-inch square.
4. Nail the tower to the flight deck, and then glue the flight deck to the hull (Fig. 4-18). Clamp until dry.
5. Paint the carrier grey, and decorate with the runway pattern and a large numeral on the deck.

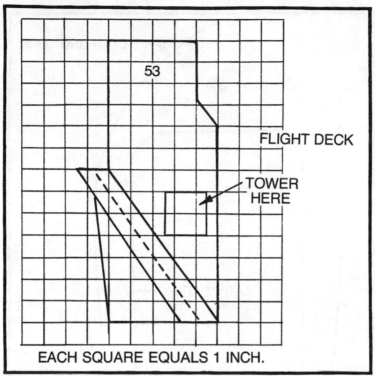

EACH SQUARE EQUALS 1 INCH.

Fig. 4-17. Trace the aircraft carrier flight deck pattern on ¼-inch thick plywood and cut out.

DINGHY

This little vessel was first used as a rowboat on the rivers of India. It is one of the easiest toys to build. No nailing or screwing is necessary.

Materials

7 inches of 1- × 4-inch pine
scrap of ¼-inch thick plywood, at least 4 × 7 inches
1-inch piece of ¼-inch diameter dowel
glue

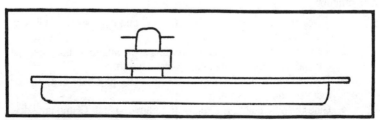

Fig. 4-18. Fasten the tower and flight deck as shown.

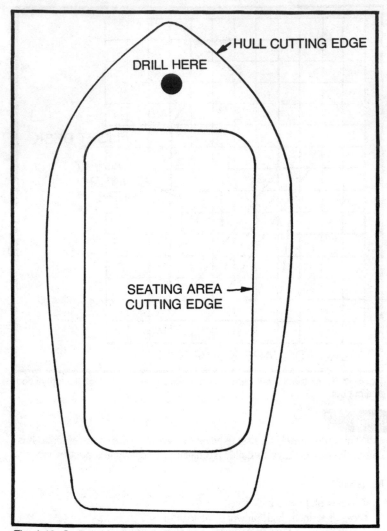

Fig. 4-19. Outline this dinghy hull on ¼-inch thick plywood.

Construction

1. Trace the hull outline on the plywood and saw out the hull (Fig. 4-19). Sand the edges smooth.
2. Trace the hull outline and the seating area outline on the pine. Cut out the hull and the opening. Sand smooth.
3. Drill a ¼-inch diameter hole through the pine hull at the point indicated on the cutting pattern.
4. Glue the pine hull to the top of the plywood hull. Clamp until dry. Glue the 1-inch piece of dowel in the predrilled hole (Fig. 4-20).

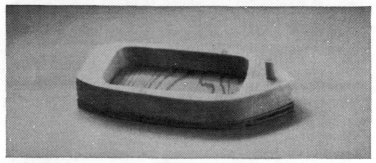

Fig. 4-20. A 1-inch dowel piece is glued in the dinghy's predrilled hole.

TUGBOAT

The hull of this tugboat, and those of the cabin cruiser and ocean liner on the following pages, are all sawn from the same cutting pattern (Fig. 4-21). Small lengths of dowel and simple blocklike shapes create the specific boat designs.

Materials

1 foot of 1- × 4-inch pine
1¼-inch piece of 2×2 lumber
3 inches of 1-inch diameter dowel
glue

Construction

1. Trace the outline of the hull on the 1- × 4-inch pine and cut out. Round off the underside of the front with a file, and then sand smooth.

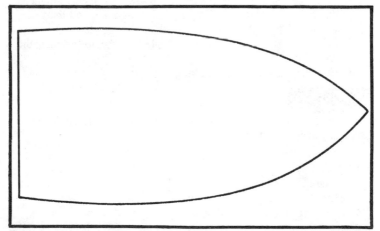

Fig. 4-21. Use this hull pattern for tugboats, cabin cruisers and ocean liners.

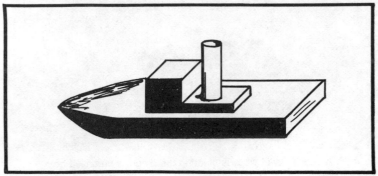

Fig. 4-22. Fasten the pieces to the hull as shown.

2. Cut out a 1½- × 2-inch piece from the 1- × 4-inch pine. Drill a 1-inch diameter hole through the center of the 1½- × 2-inch side.
3. Glue the 1½- × 2-inch piece and the 1¼-inch piece of 2×2 to the topside of the hull as shown (Fig. 4-22). Clamp until dry. Glue the dowel in the predrilled hole.

CABIN CRUISER

This neat little boat consists of two pieces—the hull and cabin. All you have to do is cut and shape the two pieces correctly and glue them together.

Materials

1 foot of 1- × 4-inch pine
glue

Construction

1. Trace the hull pattern on the pine, and saw out the hull. Round off the underside of the front of the hull with a file, and then sand smooth.
2. Cut a 2 × 2¾-inch piece of pine. Angle one edge to resemble the cabin in Fig. 4-23.
3. Glue the cabin to the hull. Clamp until dry.

OCEAN LINER

This vessel is slightly more complicated than the other. Yet it should not pose any major problem.

Materials

8½ inches of 2×4 lumber
6 inches of ½-×4-inch pine
4 inches of 1-inch diameter dowel
glue
paint

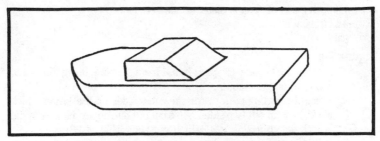

Fig. 4-23. Use this diagram to aid you in angling a cabin edge.

Construction

1. Trace the hull outline on the 2×4 and saw out. Round off the undersides of both ends with a plane or file, and sand smooth.
2. Cut the ½-inch-thick pine into two rectangles: one 2 × 5 inches, and the other 1½ × 3½ inches. Drill shallow ¼-inch diameter holes around the ½-inch edge of both rectangles to resemble port holes.
3. Center the smaller rectangle over the larger and glue the two together. Clamp until dry. When dry, drill two 1-inch diameter holes through both rectangles.
4. Glue the rectangles to the hull. Cut the 1-inch diameter dowel into two 2-inch pieces, and glue them into the predrilled holes.
5. Paint a stripe around each smokestack and a name on either side of the hull (Fig. 4-24).

FERRY BOAT

This boat will complete your son's small fleet.

Materials

1 foot of 1- × 4-inch pine
scrap of ¼-inch-thick wood, approximately 6 × 6 inches

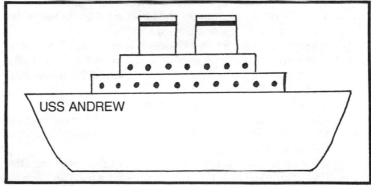

Fig. 4-24. The USS Andrew is ready to "sail."

1¼-inch piece of ½-inch diameter dowel
4d finishing nails
glue

Construction

1. Saw out the hull and the pilot house from the pine, using Fig. 4-25. Sand the edges smooth.
2. Trace the cutting pattern for the cabin sides on the ¼-inch thick wood, and cut out two sides. Also cut out one upper deck from the ¼-inch wood: a 2¼- × 4½-inch rectangle (Fig. 4-26).
3. Drill ½-inch diameter holes for windows in the cabin sides and pilot house. Also drill a ½-inch diameter hole through the pilot house to accomodate the "smokestack."
4. Nail the pilot house to the upper deck, and the upper deck to the sides. Glue the dowel in the smokestack hole in the pilot house. Nail the assembly to the hull (Fig. 4-27).

TANK

The turret with its gun revolves 360° so that the tank can "fire" in any direction.

Materials

9½ inches of 2×4 lumber
6 inches of 1- × 3-inch pine
1 foot of 1⅜-inch diameter pole
5 inches of 1-inch diameter dowel
5 inches of ½-inch diameter dowel
one 7d sinker nail
8d finishing nails
glue

Construction

1. Trace the tank base outline on the 1½-inch side of the 2×4, and saw the angles as illustrated (Fig. 4-28). Sand smooth.
2. Trace the cutting patterns for the turret and the tank top on the pine and cut out (Fig. 4-29). Sand smooth.
3. Bore a ½-inch diameter, ½-inch deep hole in the front ¾-inch edge of the turret. Glue a 5-inch piece of ½-inch dowel in this hole. Drill a ¼-inch diameter hole through the turret behind the ½-inch deep blind hole and perpendicular to it.
4. Glue and nail the top piece to the tank base (Fig. 4-30).
5. Attach the turret to the top piece with a 7d sinker nail inserted through the ¼-inch hole in the turret and driven into the top piece and the base.
6. Using a mitre box and saw, saw eight 1-inch-thick slices from the 1⅜-inch pole and four 1-inch-thick slices from the 1-inch dowel. Nail these wheels to the sides of the tank (Fig. 4-31).

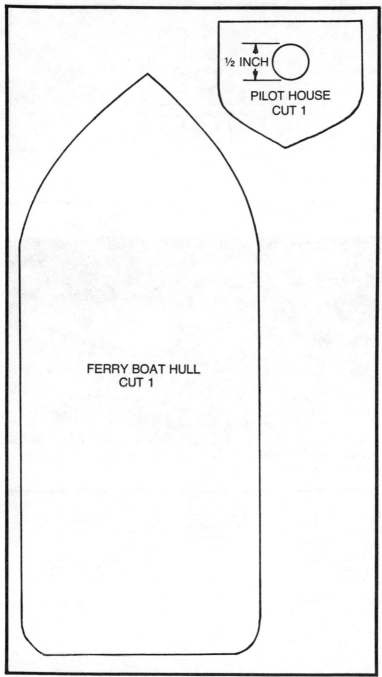

½ INCH

PILOT HOUSE
CUT 1

FERRY BOAT HULL
CUT 1

Fig. 4-25. Trace this ferry boat hull pattern on pine.

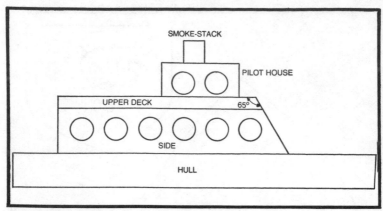

Fig. 4-26. Cut out these pieces from the ¼-inch thick board.

Fig. 4-27. After the gluing and nailing is done, your ferry boat should look something like this one.

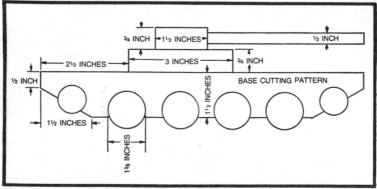

Fig. 4-28. Trace this pattern on the 1½-inch side of a 2 by 4.

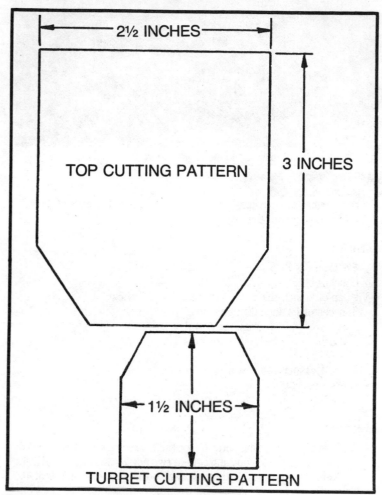

Fig. 4-29. Outline these turret and tank top patterns on pine.

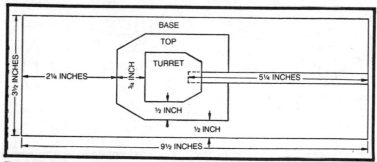

Fig. 4-30. Nail the tank pieces as shown.

Fig. 4-31. Wheels are fastened to the tank's sides.

COVERED WAGON

Your youngsters can imagine that they are back in the days of the wild west when playing with this toy.

Materials

2½ inches of 2×2
6 inches of ½- × 2-inch pine
scrap of ¼-inch-thick wood at least 4 × 8 inches
3 inches of 1¼-inch diameter pole
3 inches of ¼-inch diameter dowel
1¼ inches of ⅛-inch diameter dowel
glue
4 No. 4×1-inch roundhead screws
screw eye
twine

Construction

1. Transfer the cutting patterns for the horse and cow (Fig. 4-32) to the ¼-inch thick wood and cut out two horses and one cow. Drill a ⅛-inch diameter hole through each horse at the spot indicated.

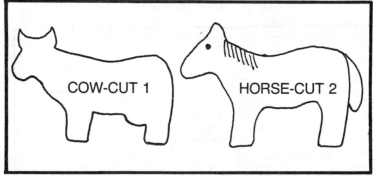

Fig. 4-32. Trace one cow and two horse patterns on ¼-inch thick wood and cut out.

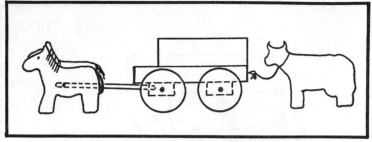

Fig. 4-33. Fasten a horse to each side of the dowel as shown.

2. Drill a ⅛-inch diameter hole through the side of a 3-inch piece of ¼-inch diameter dowel, ½ inch down from one end. Insert a 1¼-inch-long piece of ⅛-inch dowel through this hole and glue a horse to each side of the ⅛-inch dowel (Fig. 4-33).

3. Angle two edges of a 2½-inch piece of 2×2 so that it resembles the stagecoach cover illustrated (Fig. 4-34).

4. From the ½- × 2-inch piece cut a 1½- × 3-inch base piece and two 1- × 1½-inch axles.

5. Glue the cover to the base piece, flush with one end.

6. Drill a ¼-inch diameter, ¼-inch deep hole in one axle at the point indicated on the diagram (Fig. 4-35). Glue and nail this axle to the underside of the wagon front, and the second axle to the underside of the rear of the wagon.

7. Glue the ¼-inch dowel with the horses attached in the axle hole.

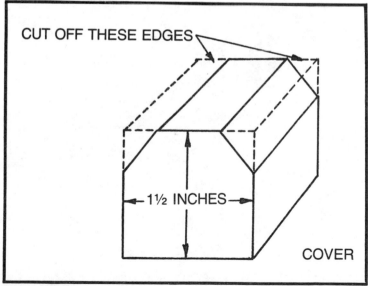

CUT OFF THESE EDGES

1½ INCHES

COVER

Fig. 4-34. Use this illustration when angling edges of a 2½-inch piece of 2 by 2.

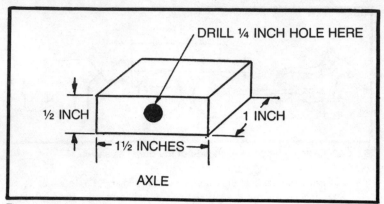

Fig. 4-35. Bore a hole in the wagon's axle as illustrated.

8. Cut four ¼-inch thick slices of 1¼-inch diameter pole. Drill a ⅛-inch hole through the center of each circle, and attach them to the axles with the roundhead screws.

9. Attach a screw eye to the end of the wagon base. Tie one end of a length of twine around the cow's neck and the other end to the screw eye.

5

Toys for Playing House

In case you were beginning to think that this book is devoted exclusively to the making of wooden toys for boys, this chapter should lay those worries to rest. Most little girls spend hours at one of their favorite pastimes—playing house. With this fact in mind, we have written a section describing the building of house appliance toys and doll playthings.

Eleven items are included in this chapter. For your daughter's doll, you can build a cradle, carriage, high chair, bed, wardrobe and house. For the experienced woodworker, there are instructions on constructing a ranch-style dollhouse. Or try objects like the oven, refrigerator, kitchen sink and washer/dryer. These toys are very realistic in appearance. Perhaps Mother might even be jealous!

DOLL CRADLE

The doll cradle has an attractive design.

Materials

    2 feet of 1×12-inch pine
    2 feet of 1×6-inch pine
    scrap of ⅜-inch plywood, 6½×12 inches
    8d finishing nails
    green paint
    varnish

Construction

1. Enlarge the cutting patterns for the headboard and footboard, and cut out one of each from the 1×12 inch pine. Sand the edges smooth (Figs. 5-1 and 5-2).

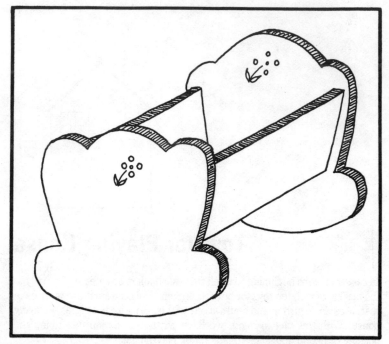

Fig. 5-1. Here is the doll cradle complete with headboard and footboard.

2. Cut the 2 feet of 1×6-inch pine in half to form two 12 inch long pieces. Sand the rough edges.
3. Drill the flower cutouts on the headboard and footboard (see Fig. 5-2). Smooth out with a circular file.
4. For the cradle bottom, cut a 6½×12-inch piece of ⅜-inch plywood and drop it into the cradle. Push it firmly in place (Figs. 5-3 and 5-4).
5. Paint on the leaves and stems with green paint (Fig. 5-5).
6. Varnish (Fig. 5-6).

DOLL HIGH CHAIR

Your child can raise and lower the tray of this high chair—just like a real one (Figs. 5-7 and 5-8).

Materials

6 feet of 1×8 inch pine
15 inches of ¾-inch diameter dowel
two No. 8 inch×2½-inch screws
3d and 8d finishing nails
paint or varnish

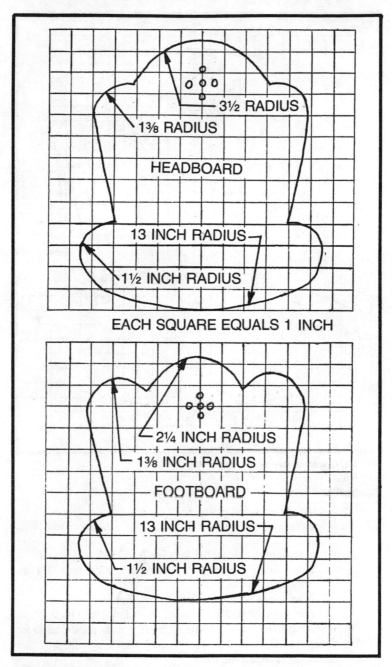

Fig. 5-2. Enlarge the headboard and footboard patterns and cut one of each out of the pine.

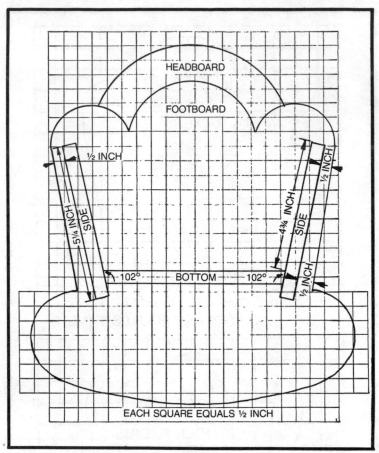

Fig. 5-3. Assemble the pieces as shown.

Construction

1. Cut out the following pieces from the pine:
   backrest—one piece 7¼ inches×8 inches (use Fig. 5-9)
   seat—one rectangle 6½ inches×7¼ inches
   sides—two rectangles with rounded corners 7¼ inches×15½ inches
   brace—one square 7¼ inches×7¼ inches
   tray—one piece 2½ inches×10½ inches (use Fig. 5-10).

2. Using Fig. 5-11 as a guide, with 8d finishing nails, nail the backrest to the seat. Next, nail the sides to the backrest and the seat. Nail the brace between the sides.

3. Cut two 7½-inch long pieces of ¾-inch diameter dowel. Drill one 3/16 inch diameter hole through each dowel, ¾-inches in from one

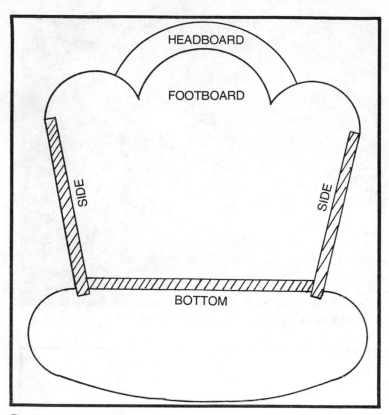

Fig. 5-4. Attach the bottom carefully.

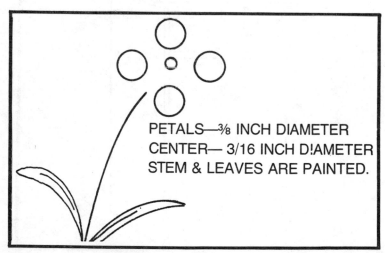

PETALS—⅜ INCH DIAMETER
CENTER— 3/16 INCH D!AMETER
STEM & LEAVES ARE PAINTED.

Fig. 5-5. Use green paint for the leaves and stems.

Fig. 5-6. This cradle is completed and already in use.

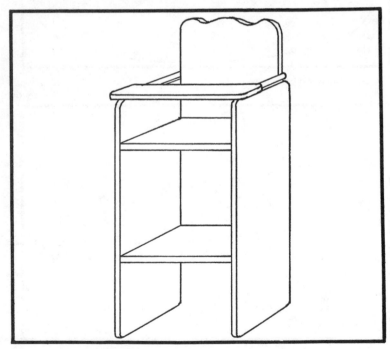

Fig. 5-7. An example of what the high chair looks like when finished.

Fig. 5-8. The high chair features a movable tray.

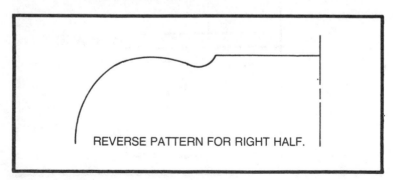

REVERSE PATTERN FOR RIGHT HALF.

Fig. 5-9. Trace this backrest pattern on the pine.

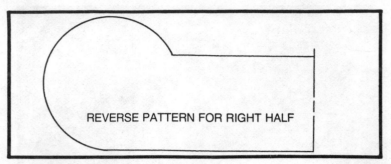

REVERSE PATTERN FOR RIGHT HALF

Fig. 5-10. Outline the tray on the pine.

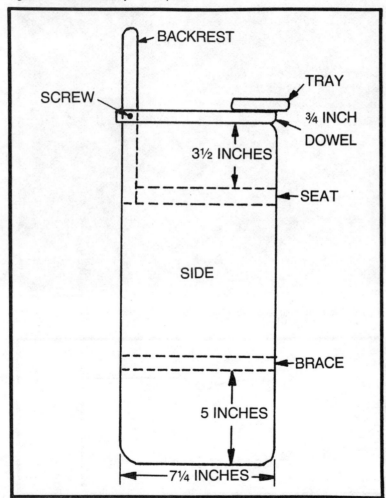

BACKREST

TRAY

SCREW

¾ INCH

DOWEL

3½ INCHES

SEAT

SIDE

BRACE

5 INCHES

7¼ INCHES

Fig. 5-11. Assemble the high chair parts as illustrated.

end. Insert a screw through each hole and screw a dowel to either side of the backrest.

4. Center the tray over the dowels, and nail it to the dowels with the 3d finishing nails.
5. Sand smooth, and either paint or varnish (Fig. 5-12).

Fig. 5-12. This doll enjoys her new high chair.

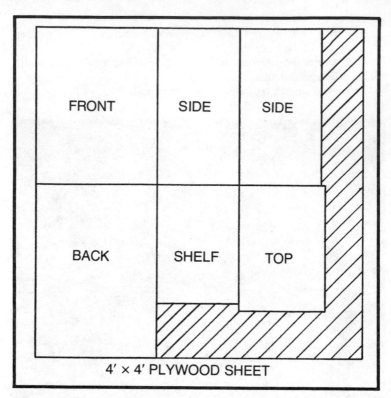

FRONT SIDE SIDE

BACK SHELF TOP

4' × 4' PLYWOOD SHEET

Fig. 5-13. All the dollhouse pieces are cut out of 4 by 4 foot plywood.

DOLL HOUSE

All homes should be sturdy. This doll house, if built properly, will be no exception.

Materials

4×4 feet sheet of ⅜ inch interior A-A plywood
4d finishing nails
glue
primer and paint

Construction

1. Saw out the following pieces from the plywood (Fig. 5-13):
    front—one piece, 29¾×20 inches (use Fig. 5-14)
    floors—three rectangles, 19¼ inches×8¼ inches
    roof—two rectangles, 16×9¼ inches and 15⅝ inches×9¼ inches
    sides—two rectangles, 20¼×8¼ inches: bevel top

8¼ inches edge 45 degrees
partition—one rectangle, 9¼×8¼ inches
roof supports—one strip 8¼×1¾ inches and
one strip 8¼×1⅜ inches

2. Using Fig. 5-15 as a guide, glue and nail the sides to the bottom and top floors. Attach the partition to the middle floor and glue and nail it to the house. Glue and nail the front to the sides and three floors.
3. The roof is put on so that it is flush with the back of the house and overhangs the front Fig. 5-16. Glue one roof strip to each roof piece, ⅜ inches down from the peak edge and flush with the edge of

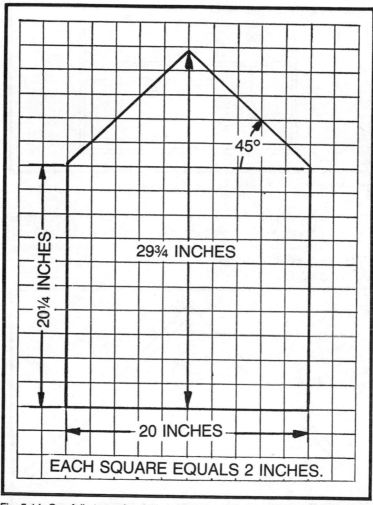

Fig. 5-14. Carefully trace the dollhouse front pattern on the plywood.

113

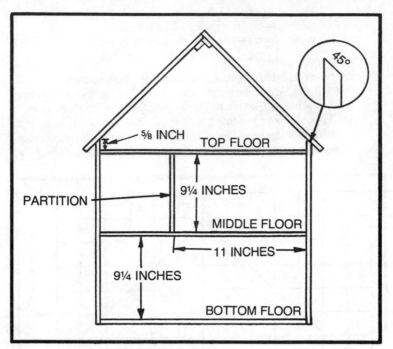

Fig. 5-15. Assemble the dollhouse pieces as shown.

the roof that will be at the back of the house. Use the wider strip on the larger roof piece. Glue and nail the roof to the sides and front.

4. Prime and then paint. Decorate the front of the house with doors, windows, shutters, shrubbery, flowers, etc. Fig. 5-18.

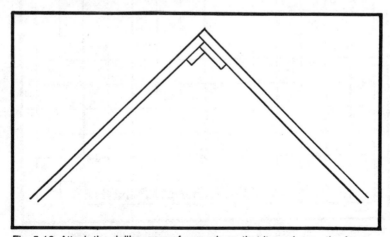

Fig. 5-16. Attach the dollhouse roof properly so that it overhangs the front.

Fig. 5-17. Susan's house is ready for occupants.

DOLL CARRIAGE

Every doll needs a doll buggy. This little vehicle will take your girl's doll wherever it wants to go.

Materials

3×4 sheet of ½ A-A plywood
6-feet of 1×2
¾ inch diameter dowel, 12 inches long
four ¼×3½ inch lag screws, 8 washers
flat head screws, finishing nails, glue
paint, varnish

Construction

1. Using Figs. 5-18 through 5-21, saw out the components and smooth the edges.

Fig. 5-18. Several cutting patterns are used to construct this carriage.

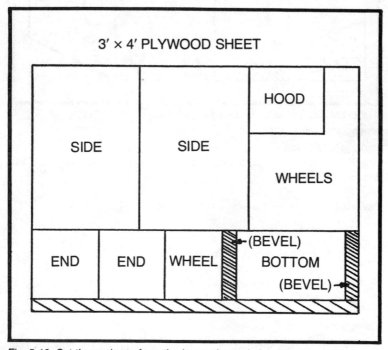

Fig. 5-19. Cut these pieces from the large plywood sheet.

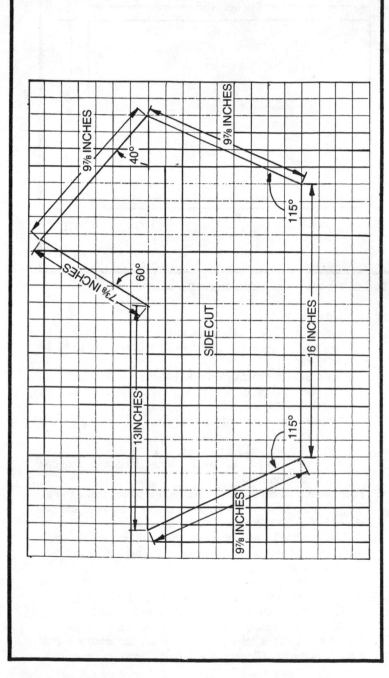

Fig. 5-20. Use this pattern to trace the carriage sides. Each square equals one inch.

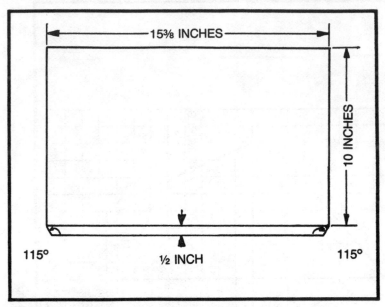

Fig. 5-21. Outline this bottom pattern on the plywood.

From the plywood cut:
  sides—two pieces 24¼×15⅜ inches
  ends—two rectangles—10¼×10 inches and 10⅛×10 inches
  hood top—one rectangle 9⅞×11 inches
  bottom—one piece 10×15⅜ inches with each 10 inch side beveled 115 degrees
  wheels—four 6 inch diameter circles.
From the 1×2 cut:
  axle—two pieces 13 inches long
  side handles—two pieces 21 inches long with rounded corners on one end.

2. Place the end pieces in position on the side pieces (refer to Fig. 5-22), and mark and cut the bottom edges at the proper angle as shown in Fig. 5-23. Nail the sides to the ends.

3. Position the hood top (Fig. 5-22), and mark and cut the angle where the hood top meets the end piece as shown in Fig. 5-24. Nail the hood top to the sides.

4. Attach the bottom with glue and nails.

5. Hold the side handles against the sides of the buggy (Fig. 5-22), and mark and cut the bottom edge at the proper angle.

6. Round all sharp corners of the buggy by sanding.

7. Bore ¾ inch diameter holes ½ inch deep in the side handles, ¾ inch down from the top. Glue the ¾ inch dowel between these holes.

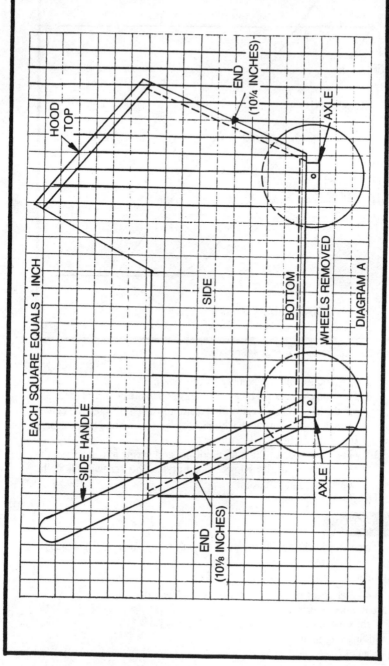

Fig. 5-22. This diagram illustrates placement of end pieces and side pieces.

119

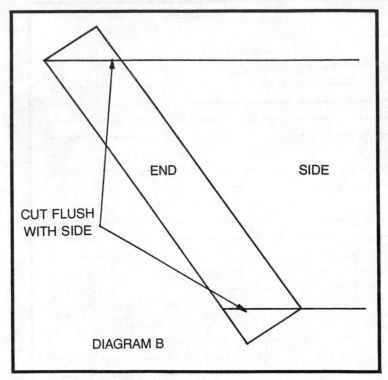

SIDE

END

CUT FLUSH
WITH SIDE

DIAGRAM B

Fig. 5-23. Cut the bottom edges properly.

8. Screw the handle assembly to the sides.
9. Drill ¼ inch diameter holes 2 inches deep in the center of each axle for the lag screws. Drill ¼ inch diameter holes through the center of each wheel. Screw on wheels with lag screws and two washers (see Fig. 5-25).
10. Glue 1×2 axles to the buggy bottom and screw in place from the bottom piece of the buggy. Countersink the screws, fill in the holes, and sand smooth.
11. Paint or varnish.

TOY OVEN

The off/on knobs on this toy oven actually turn (Figs. 5-26 and 5-27).

Materials

4×4 feet sheet of ⅜ inch interior A-C plywood
four wooden cabinet knobs
eight washers that will fit the knobs' screws
4d finishing nails
paint

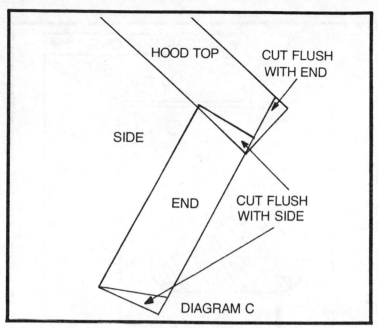

Fig. 5-24. Use this illustration for help in cutting the angle where the hood top and end piece connect.

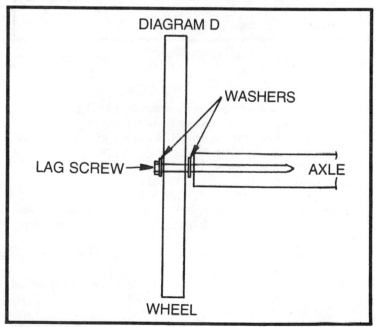

Fig. 5-25. Screw on the wheels with lag screws and washers as shown.

Fig. 5-26. Susan's stove is ready for "cooking."

Construction

1. Cut out the following panels from the plywood (Fig. 5-27):
   sides—two rectangles 12×23 inches
   front—one rectangle 18×23 inches with a 9×12 inch opening (use Fig. 5-29)
   back—one rectangle 18×25 inches
   top—one rectangle 12⅜×18 inches
   shelf—one rectangle 12×17¼ inches.
2. Drill four holes through the front panel and screw on the knobs. Use a washer on either side of the plywood so the knobs will turn "off" and "on."
3. Nail the sides to the front and back pieces. Nail the horizontal shelf in place (Fig. 5-29).
4. Glue and nail the top flush with the front and side edges, so that it is resting against the back panel (Fig. 5-29).
5. Round off all sharp edges by sanding.
6. Prime and paint the stove. Paint four "burners" on the top piece, along with whatever other decorations you wish.

You will have a lot of left-over plywood at the end of this project. A 4×4 foot piece is too small for the job though (Fig. 5-31).

Fig. 5-27. The stove's on/off knobs actually turn.

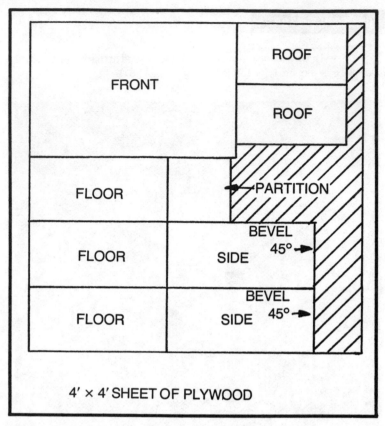

Fig. 5-28. These oven pieces are cut from interior A-C plywood.

Material

4×8 foot sheet of ⅜-inch interior A-C plywood
two 1-inch diameter knobs
two sets of magnetic door catches
4d finishing nails
paint or varnish

Construction

1. Cut out the following pieces from the plywood:
   back—one rectangle 14×30 inches
   sides—two rectangles 12×30 inches
   shelves—three rectangles 12×13¼ inches
   top—one rectangle 12⅜×14 inches
   freezer door—one rectangle 10⅜×14 inches
   refrigerator door—one rectangle 14×17 inches

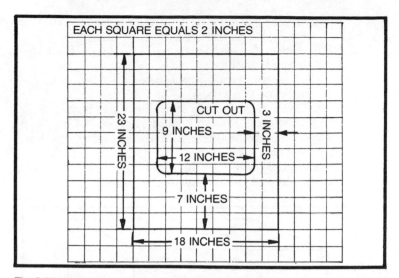

Fig. 5-29. Trace this oven front pattern on the plywood.

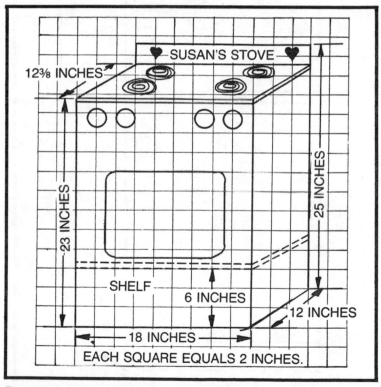

Fig. 5-30. Fasten the oven pieces as illustrated.

separator strips—one rectangle 1×14 inches
—one rectangle 2×14 inches.

2. Nail the back to the sides, and the top to the sides and back (see Fig. 5-32 for steps 2-6).
3. Nail the three horizontal shelves between the side pieces.
4. Screw the knobs to the doors.
5. Nail the 2-inch separator strip across the bottom front.
6. Attach the hinges and hang the refrigerator door. Nail the 1-inch separator strip across the front, right above the refrigerator door. Hang the freezer door.
7. Mount magnetic catches for the doors.
8. Sand any sharp edges, and then paint or varnish.

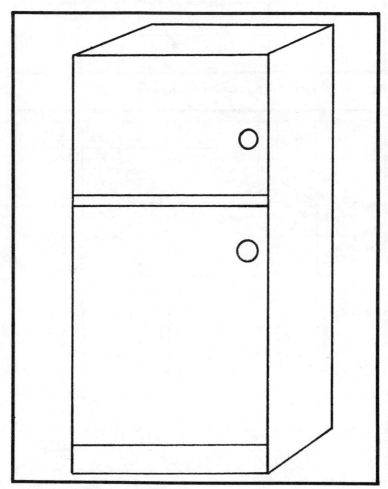

Fig. 5-31. A completed toy refrigerator.

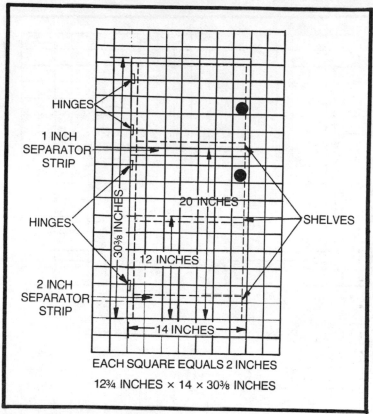

EACH SQUARE EQUALS 2 INCHES

12¾ INCHES × 14 × 30⅜ INCHES

Fig. 5-32. Fasten the refrigerator parts together as shown.

TOY WASHER AND DRYER

Your daughter's playhouse would not be complete without this beautiful laundry center.

Materials

4×8 foot sheet of ⅜-inch A-C interior plywood
four 2-inch diameter knobs
eight washers to fit the screws of the knobs
4d finishing nails
black paint
varnish

Construction

1. Saw out the following pieces from the plywood:
   front—one rectangle 22×28 inches with a 10-inch diameter circular opening (use Fig. 5-33)

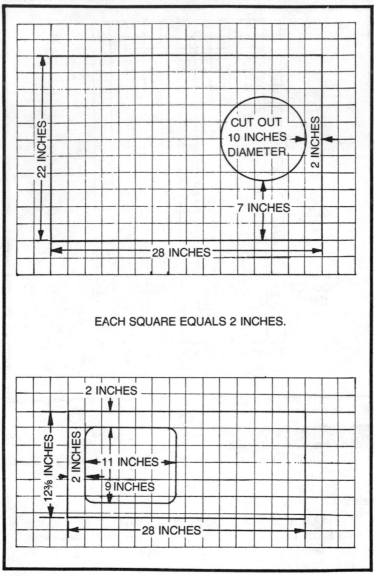

EACH SQUARE EQUALS 2 INCHES.

Fig. 5-33. Outline the washer and dryer front and top patterns carefully.

sides and vertical divider—three rectangles 12×22 inches

back—one rectangle 24×28 inches

top—one rectangle 12⅜×28 inches, with a 9×11 inch opening

(use Fig. 5-33)

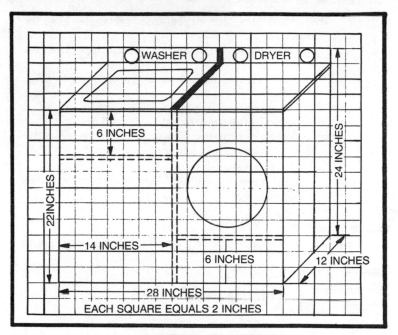

Fig. 5-34. Assemble the laundry center parts as shown.

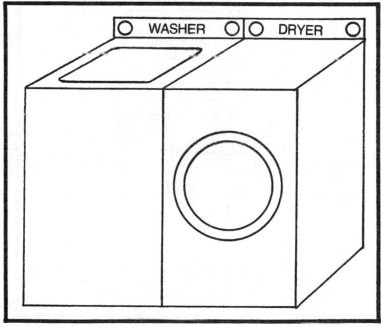

Fig. 5-35. A finished washer and dryer.

horizontal shelf for dryer—one rectangle 12×13¼ inches

horizontal shelf for washer—one rectangle 12×13⅝ inches.

2. Nail the sides and the vertical divider to the front and back (see Fig. 5-34 for steps 2-5).
3. Nail the horizontal shelves in place.
4. Nail the top so that it is flush with the sides and front.
5. Attach the four knobs to the back with washers on either side of the plywood in order for the knobs to turn.
6. Sand all sharp edges smooth.
7. Paint a black stripe between the washer and dryer to define the two. Varnish (Fig. 5-35).

TOY KITCHEN SINK

Nine panels will be sawed out of the plywood to build this kitchen sink.

Materials

4×8 foot sheet of ⅜-inch interior A-C plywood
scrap of 1 inch pine

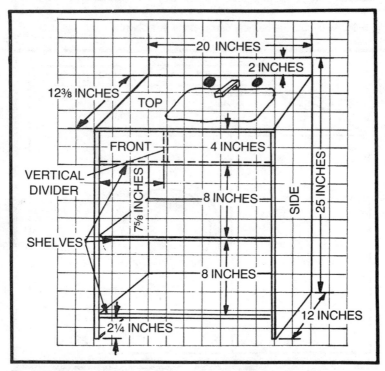

Fig. 5-36. These pieces must all be cut from the interior plywood.

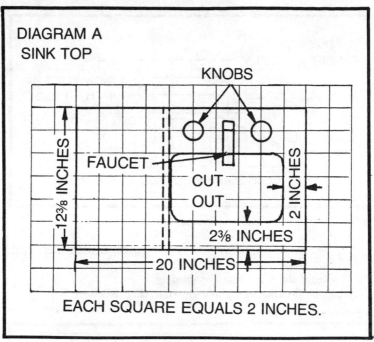

DIAGRAM A
SINK TOP

KNOBS

FAUCET

CUT
OUT

12⅜ INCHES

2 INCHES

2⅜ INCHES

20 INCHES

EACH SQUARE EQUALS 2 INCHES.

Fig. 5-37. Construct the sink top as shown.

two 2 inch diameter knobs
six washers sized to fit the screws of the knobs
4d finishing nails
glue
one No. 6×2 inch flathead screw
paint

Construction

1. Cut out the following panels from the plywood (Fig. 5-36):
   top—one rectangle 12⅜×20 inches with a 6×10 inch opening (Fig. 5-37)
   back—one rectangle 20×25 inches
   sides—two rectangles 12×23 inches
   front—one rectangle 4×20 inches
   horizontal shelves—three rectangles 12×19¼ inches
   vertical divider—one rectangle 3⅜×12 inches.
2. Glue and nail the front and back to the sides. Next, nail the vertical partition to the top horizontal shelf. Then, nail the horizontal shelves in place.
3. Assemble the faucet by following (Fig. 5-39). Screw the knobs and faucet to the top piece, using washers on either side of the plywood.

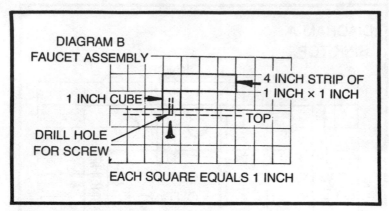

DIAGRAM B
FAUCET ASSEMBLY

4 INCH STRIP OF
1 INCH × 1 INCH

1 INCH CUBE

TOP

DRILL HOLE
FOR SCREW

EACH SQUARE EQUALS 1 INCH

Fig. 5-38. Assemble the faucet as illustrated.

4. Nail the top with the knobs and faucet in place to the sides, front, and back.
5. Round the sharp edges by sanding.
6. Paint the counter top a bright color (Fig. 5-39).

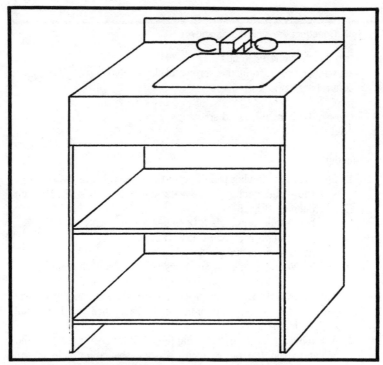

Fig. 5-39. After painting the counter top, the sink is finished.

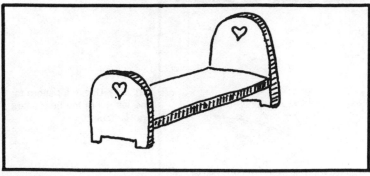

Fig. 5-40. This completed doll bed includes a heart shape in the headboard and footboard.

This attractive toy will make a comfortable resting place for your little girl's dolls. Three pieces comprise the bed (Fig. 5-40).

Materials

3 foot of 1×8 inch pine
8d finishing nails
paint or varnish (optional)

Construction

1. Draw a cutting pattern for the headboard and footboard, using Figs. 5-41 and 5-42.
2. From the pine cut:
   one base—7¼×15 inch rectangle
   one headboard—7¼×8¾ inches
   one footboard—7¼×7¾ inches (Fig. 5-43)

Fig. 5-41. This pattern is for the top left side of the headboard and footboard.

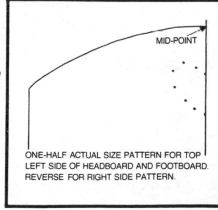

ONE-HALF ACTUAL SIZE PATTERN FOR TOP LEFT SIDE OF HEADBOARD AND FOOTBOARD. REVERSE FOR RIGHT SIDE PATTERN.

133

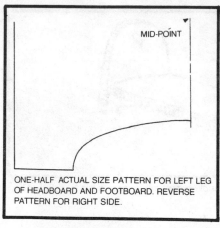

MID-POINT

Fig. 5-42. Use this pattern for the left leg of the headboard and footboard.

ONE-HALF ACTUAL SIZE PATTERN FOR LEFT LEG OF HEADBOARD AND FOOTBOARD. REVERSE PATTERN FOR RIGHT SIDE.

3. Drill 1/16 inch diameter holes in the headboard and footboard to form the shape of a heart.
4. Sand the three pieces smooth.
5. With 8d finishing nails, nail the headboard and footboard to the base, so that the base is 3 inches from the floor (Fig. 5-44).
6. Paint or varnish if you wish.

RANCH-STYLE DOLL HOUSE

This elaborate doll house will require some patience in building. You will need both plywood and balsa strip (Fig. 5-45).

Materials

3×4 foot sheet of A-A plywood
17 feet of 1/16×½ inch balsa strip

6d finishing nails
glue

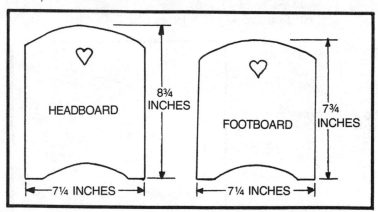

Fig. 5-43. Cut one headboard and footboard from the pine with these dimensions.

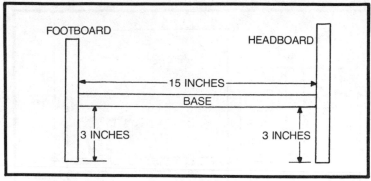

Fig. 5-44. Assemble the doll bed pieces as shown.

Construction

1. Using Fig. 5-46 as a guide, cut out the following pieces from the plywood:
   side A—6½×19 inches
   side AA—6½×19 inches
   side B—6½×22 inches
   side BB—6½×22 inches
   base—18½×22 inches
   divider C—2×6 inches
   divider D—2½×6 inches
   divider E—3×6 inches—cut two
   divider F—4½×6 inches
   divider G—6×7 inches
   divider H—6×9 inches.

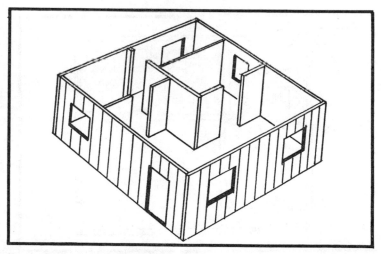

Fig. 5-45. This ranch-style dollhouse is one of the most complicated toys.

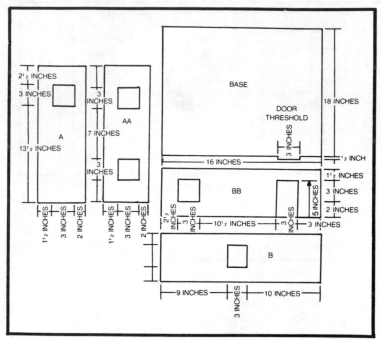

Fig. 5-46. Trace these ranch-style dollhouse patterns on plywood and saw out.

2. With an awl, draw vertical lines 1 inch apart on the outsides of pieces A, AA, B, and BB to resemble vertical siding. Draw vertical lines ½ inch apart on the topside of the base to resemble plank flooring (see Fig. 5-47 for steps 2-7).

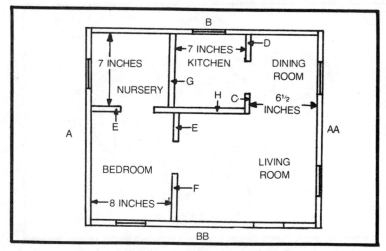

Fig. 5-47. Glue and nail the sides, base and divider, as the diagram illustrates.

3. Glue and nail sides B and BB between sides A and AA.
4. Glue and nail the base inside the assembled sides so that the door threshold fits into the doorway.
5. Glue and nail the room dividers in place.
6. Glue balsa strips cut to fit to the inside of the windows and doorway to frame them.
7. Glue balsa strips cut to fit to the top of the outside and inside walls to cover the exposed plywood eges.

DOLL WARDROBE

Your daughter will put this closet to good use. It has plenty of shelf space for your daughter to place the doll clothes (Fig. 5-48).

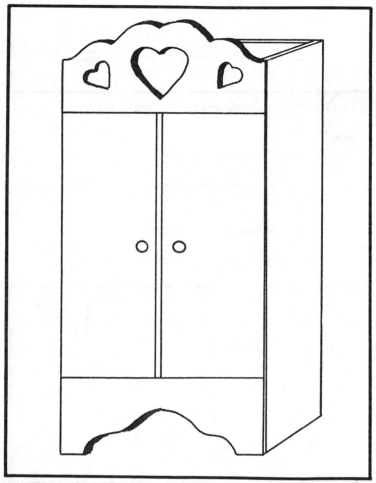

Fig. 5-48. The doll wardrobe may be painted to enhance its appearance.

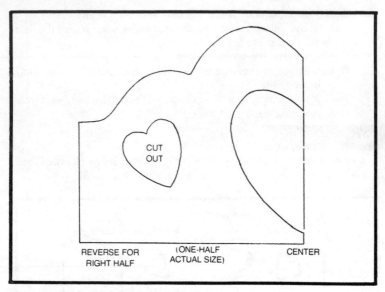

Fig. 5-49. The doll wardrobe top front piece cutting pattern.

Materials

38 inches of ½×10 inch pine
53 inches of ½×8 inch pine
8¾ inch length of ½-inch diameter dowel
6d finishing nails
glue
four ⅜×1 inch butt hinges with screws
two small knobs
paint or varnish (optional)

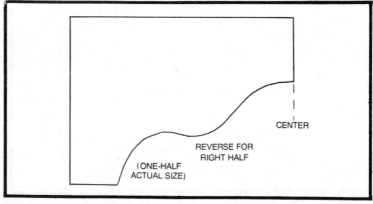

Fig. 5-50. The doll wardrobe bottom front piece cutting pattern.

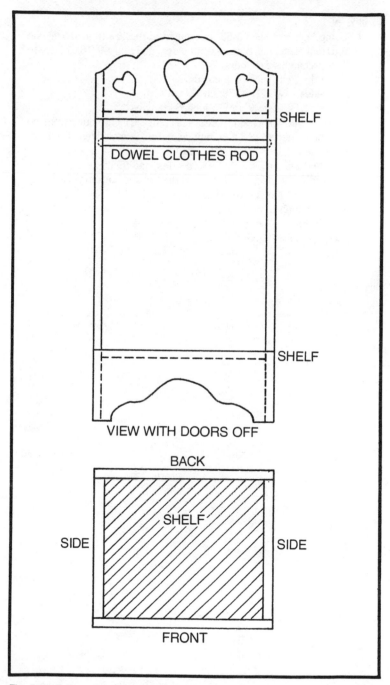

SHELF

DOWEL CLOTHES ROD

SHELF

VIEW WITH DOORS OFF

BACK

SHELF

SIDE

SIDE

FRONT

Fig. 5-51. Fasten the doll wardrobe pieces as shown.

139

Construction

1. Using Figs. 5-49 and 5-50, cut out from the ½×10-inch pine one top front piece, one bottom front piece, and two 4-9/16×11-15/16 inch rectangles for doors.
2. From the ½×8-inch pine cut out:
   sides—two 7¼×18-inch rectangles
   shelves—two 7¼×8¾ inch rectangles.
3. On the inside of each side piece, at a point 2½ inches down from the top and centered, drill a ½ inch diameter, ¼ inch deep blind hole. Glue the 8⅜ inch piece of ½-inch dowel in these holes.
4. Glue and nail the back to the two sides, and then glue and nail the two shelves in place. Glue and nail the top and bottom front pieces to the sides and shelves (Fig. 5-51).
5. Screw a knob to each door.
6. Attach the hinges and hang the doors.
7. Paint or varnish if you wish.

Toys to Play On

Any department store employee who works in the toy section will tell you that riding toys, or toys to play on, are adored by children. Every boy and girl dreams about the day when he or she gets that first bicycle or tricycle. You can make a beautiful wooden bike for your toddler which will keep him or her happy until you feel that a new, standard bike is both appropriate and within your budget.

If your children would like another animal toy, make a riding hen or other type of bird. The hobbyhorse and rocking horse are old favorites that are relatively easy to build. There are also instructions for constructing a rocking chair, stilts and a crawl-in cube. If built properly, all these toys are safe and ideal for your kids. You will need some pine, dowel pieces and finishing nails for the production of these toys.

HOBBYHORSE

Little children especially girls, are charmed by horses. This hobbyhorse is a snap to construct and will give the kids hours of riding pleasure.

Materials

    1 foot of 1×10-inch clear pine
    42 inches of ¾ inch diameter dowel
    8d finishing nails
    glue
    paint

Construction

    1. Enlarge Fig. 6-1 on paper, transfer them to the pine, and saw out one horse's head and two braces. Sand smooth.

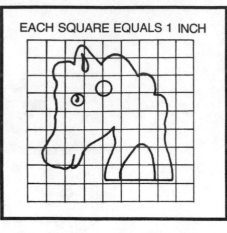

EACH SQUARE EQUALS 1 INCH

Fig. 6-1. Trace the enlarged hobbyhorse pattern on the clear pine.

2. Drill a ¾-inch diameter hole through the head for the handle. Drill a blind hole ¾ inches in diameter to a depth of 1½ inches at the center point of the bottom edge of the head (Fig. 6-2).
3. Nail the braces to either side of the head.
4. Cut the ¾-inch diameter dowel into one 7-inch length and one 36-inch length. Sand both ends of the 7 inch piece, and one end of the 36 inch piece. Insert the 7 inch piece through the head so that there is an equal amount on either side of the head, and glue it in place. Glue the rough end of the 36-inch piece on the blind hole.
5. Paint features (Fig. 6-3 and 6-4).

ROCKING HORSE

If the youngsters get tired of the hobbyhorse, this rocking horse is an enjoyable alternative. Please make certain to position the legs on the crossbraces correctly.

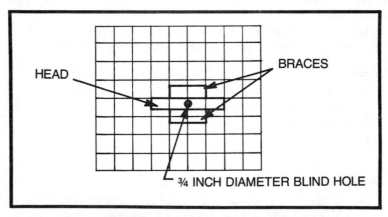

HEAD

BRACES

¾ INCH DIAMETER BLIND HOLE

Fig. 6-2. Use this illustration to guide you in drilling holes in the horse's head.

Materials

    8 feet of 1×12 inch pine
    7 inches of ¾ inch diameter dowel
    8d finishing nails
    glue
    paint or varnish

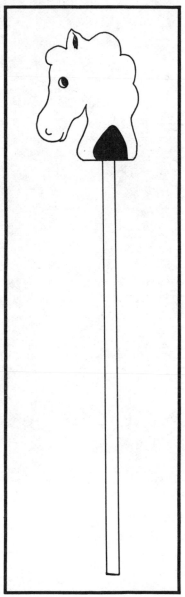

Fig. 6-3. An illustration of a completed hobbyhorse.

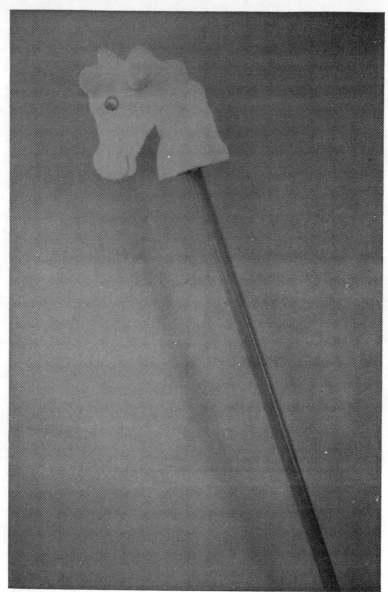

Fig. 6-4. This hobbyhorse is all set for a rider.

Construction

1. Enlarge Figs. 6-5 through 6-7, transfer them to the pine, and cut
out the following:

   head—one piece 9½×10 inches
   seat—one piece 8×15 inches

144

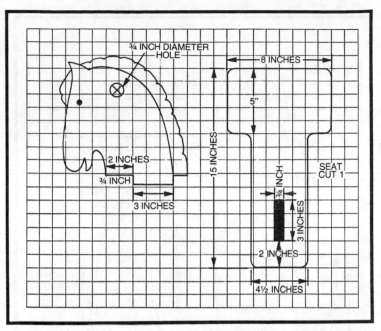

Fig. 6-5. Enlarge the rocking horse head and seat patterns. Then transfer them to the pine.

legs—two pieces 6×10 inches
stringer—one piece 3×11½ inches
rockers—two pieces 7×30 inches
crossbraces—two pieces 4×11½ inches

To minimize waste, arrange the cutting patterns for the two rockers on the pine as shown in Fig. 6-6.

2. Center the legs on the crossbraces. Glue and nail in place.
3. Mark the center point of the top of the legs. Nail the stringer between the legs at the center point. Saw the legs flush with the stringer as shown in Fig. 6-8.

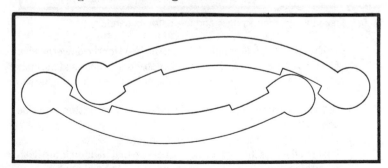

Fig. 6-6. Arrange the rockers pattern on the pine as illustrated.

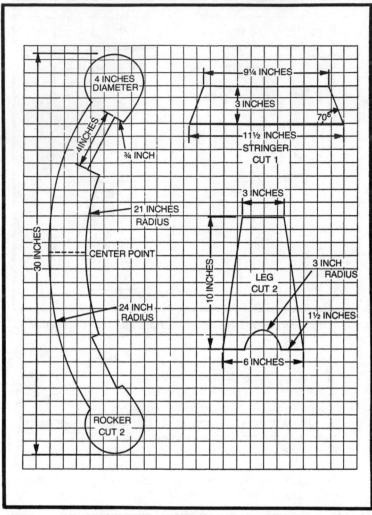

Fig. 6-7. Trace the enlarged stringer and leg patterns carefully.

4. Drill a ¾-inch diameter hole through the head for the dowel handle. Cut a 7-inch long piece of ¾-inch diameter dowel and sand the ends smooth. Insert the handle through the hole in the head and glue it in place.
5. Set the head notch into the opening in the seat and fasten with glue and nails.
6. Nail the seat to the legs and the stringer.
7. Position the crossbraces on the rockers so that their ends are flush with the outer edges of the rockers. Glue and nail in place.
8. Paint or varnish (Fig. 6-9).

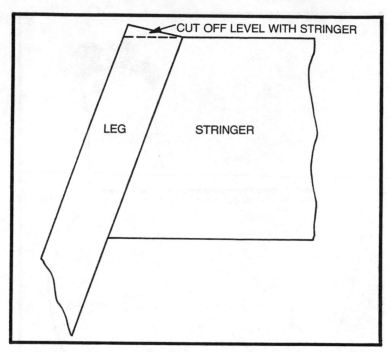

CUT OFF LEVEL WITH STRINGER

LEG

STRINGER

Fig. 6-8. When cutting the horse's legs, be sure they are flush with the stringer.

Fig. 6-9. The completed horse is ready for rocking.

Fig. 6-10. The riding hen is only one of many birds that you can build.

RIDING HEN

By substituting a different head, you can make just about any kind of bird you want—a swan, a cardinal, a blue jay—whatever strikes your fancy (Fig. 6-10).

Materials

3 feet of 1×10-inch pine
2 feet of 1×8-inch pine
3 feet of 1×6-inch pine
8d finishing nails
glue

four flat-plate swivel casters with 1⅝-inch wheels and mounting screws
white, red, yellow, blue and black paint

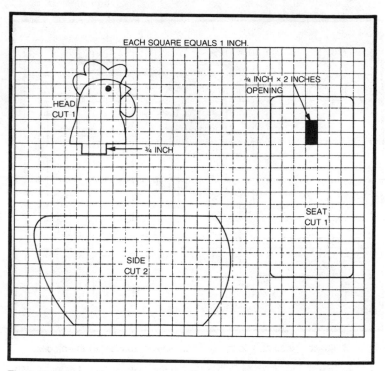

Fig. 6-11. Enlarge all patterns, trace, and cut two sides, one head and one seat from the pine.

Construction

1. Enlarge Fig. 6-11 for the head, sides, and seat. Cut two sides from the 1×10-inch pine. From the 1×8-inch pine cut one seat and one head. From the 1×6-inch pine, cut one 5¼×11-inch rectangle for the base, two 5¼×8-inch rectangles for the ends, and one tail (Fig. 6-12) (optional). Sand rough edges.

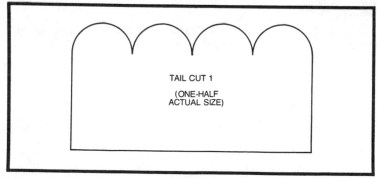

Fig. 6-12. Outline and cut the optional tail carefully.

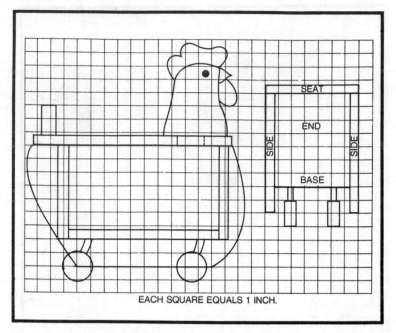

EACH SQUARE EQUALS 1 INCH.

Fig. 6-13. Attach the casters to the base as shown and fasten the pieces.

2. Screw one caster to each corner of the base, at a point ½ inch down and ½ inch across from the corner (Fig. 6-13).
3. Nail the ends to the base.
4. Position the head in the slot on the seat, and glue the head to the seat. Attach the tail (optional) to the seat with glue and nails.
5. Nail the ends to the seat and the sides to the seat, ends, and base (Fig. 6-13).
6. Sand and prime. Paint the body and head white, the combs red, the beak yellow, the eyes blue, and the wing outline black.

TOT'S BIKE

This toy is ideal for the pre-school child. Your tot can use this bike to practice on until he's ready for a full-sized tricycle.

Materials

3 feet of 1×8-inch pine
1 foot of 2×6-inch pine
6½ inches of 1-inch diameter dowel
1 of 1½-inch diameter pole
four 3-inch lag screws and 8 washers
4d and 8d finishing nails
glue
paint or varnish

Fig. 6-14. A completed riding hen.

Construction

1. Enlarge Fig. 6-15 for the seat and handle. Outline the patterns on the 1-inch pine, as well as four 3-inch diameter circles for wheels, and cut out. Drill a 1-1/16 inch diameter hole through the seat, and a 1 inch diameter hole ½-inch deep in the handle at the points

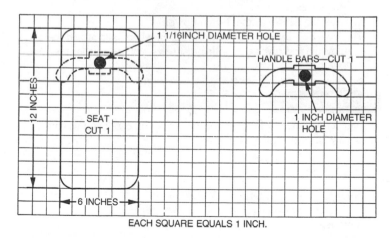

EACH SQUARE EQUALS 1 INCH.

Fig. 6-15. Enlarge and trace these bike patterns on pine.

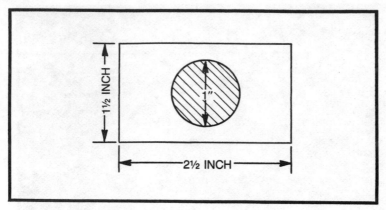

Fig. 6-16. Follow this diagram when working with the front axle.

indicated on the cutting patterns. Round off all sharp edges by sanding.

2. Cut one front axle, 2½×5½-inches and one rear axle 5×5½-inches from the 2×6-inch pine. Drill a 1-inch diameter hole 2 inches deep into the top of the front axle (refer to Fig. 6-16).

3. Insert the 6½-inch piece of 1 inch diameter dowel through the hole in the seat and glue it into the hole in the front axle. Nail the dowel and axle together with 4d finishing nails.

4. With 8d finishing nails, nail the seat to the front and rear axles, as shown in Fig. 6-17.

5. Drill a 1-inch diameter hole through the center of a 1-inch slice of 1½ inch diameter pole. Slip it down over the 1-inch diameter dowel until it rests on the seat. Glue the slice in place, and then nail it to the dowel.

6. Glue the handle to the 1-inch dowel.

7. Drill a hole through the center of each wheel, and attach them to the front and rear axles with lag screws, using a washer on either side of each wheel.

8. Paint or varnish (Fig. 6-18).

TUGBOAT ROCKER

Tugboat rockers are fairly novelistic toys. Generally you will not find rocking playthings designed as tugboats.

Materials

3×4 foot of ¾-inch interior A-A plywood
17 of ¾-inch diameter dowel
8d finishing nails
glue
paint

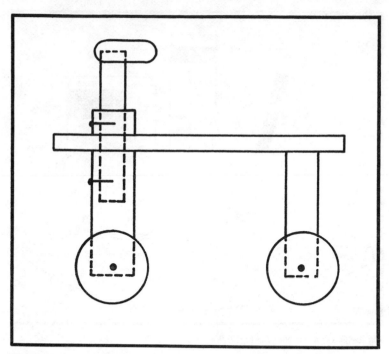

Fig. 6-17. Fasten the seat to the axles as shown here.

Construction

1. Enlarge Fig. 6-19 and Fig. 6-20 on paper. Trace the paper pattern on the plywood, and saw out two tugboats. Drill a ¾ inch diameter blind hole ½ deep on the inside of each tug at the spot indicated on the cutting pattern. Sand the cut edges smooth.
2. Also cut out from the plywood (Fig. 6-21).

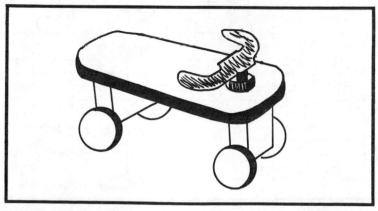

Fig. 6-18. When completed, the tot bike should look similar to this one.

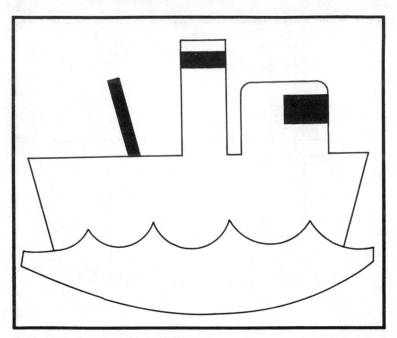

Fig. 6-19. An example of a tugboat rocker.

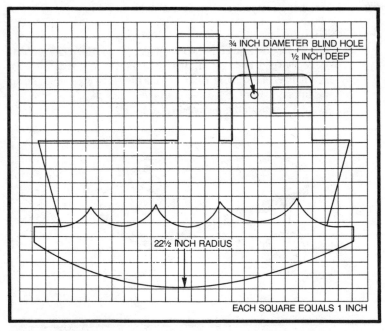

¾ INCH DIAMETER BLIND HOLE
½ INCH DEEP

22½ INCH RADIUS

EACH SQUARE EQUALS 1 INCH

Fig. 6-20. Trace and cut out two tugboats using this pattern.

154

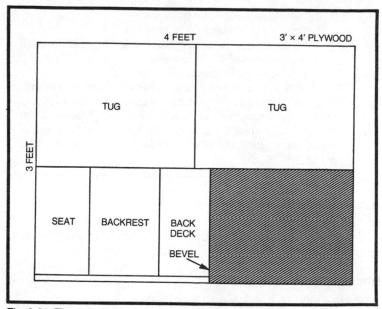

Fig. 6-21. These parts must all be cut from the plywood.

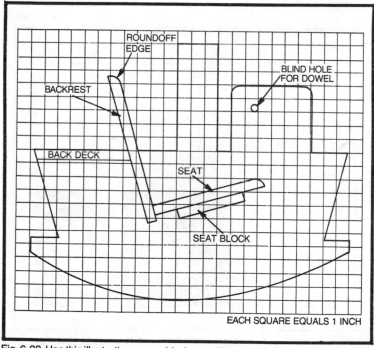

EACH SQUARE EQUALS 1 INCH

Fig. 6-22. Use this illustration as an aid when nailing the tugboat pieces together.

155

seat—one rectangle 11×16 inches
backrest—one rectangle 11×16 inches
back deck—one rectangle 6¾×16 inches, with one 16 inch edge beveled to 75 degrees
seatblocks—two rectangles ¾×5 inches

Round off the sharp edges of the seat and backrest by sanding.

3. Using Fig. 6-22 as a guide, glue and nail the seat to the backrest to form a chair. Glue and nail this chair to one tugboat. Glue the dowel between both tugboats, and then attach the second tug to the chair. Glue the two seat blocks underneath the seat for added support.

4. Nail the back deck flush with the top edges of the tugboats.

5. Paint.

CHAIR ROCKER

This rocking chair will make a nice addition to the other rocking toys. The chair is durable and should last a long time.

Materials

3×4 foot sheet of ¾ inch A-A interior plywood
17½ of ¾ inch diameter dowel
glue, and finishing nails
paint or varnish

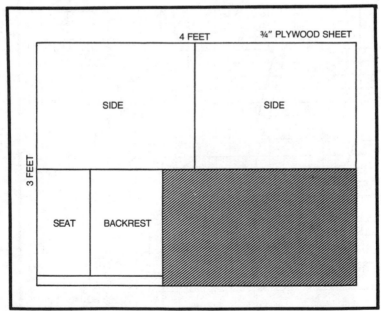

Fig. 6-23. The rocker sides, backrest, backrest supports, seat and seat supports will be traced on and sawed out of interior plywood.

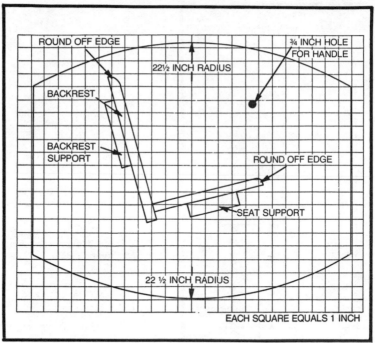

Fig. 6-24. Fasten the rocker pieces together as shown.

Construction

1. Enlarge Fig. 6-23 for the rocker sides, transfer it to the plywood, and cut out two side pieces, approximately 19×24 inches.
2. Also cut out from the plywood (Fig. 6-23):
   - backrest—one rectangle 11×16 inches
   - backrest supports—two rectangles ¾×5 inches
   - seat—one rectangle 8×16 inches
   - seat supports—two rectangles ¾×4 inches.
4. Sand all edges smooth, and round off the top edge of the backrest and the bottom edge of the seat.
4. Drill a ¾-inch diameter hole through the side pieces to accomodate a ¾ inch diameter dowel handle.
5. Nail the seat to the backrest to form a chair. (Refer to Fig. 6-24). Glue and nail the chair and the dowel between the two rockers. Glue the supports to the backrest and seat.
6. Paint if you wish. Varnish for a durable finish.

STILTS

Stilts for a child to walk on must be carefully made. To reduce the risk of slipping, the bottoms can be given rubber feet either the type used on shoe heels or pieces of sheet rubber nailed on. Check to see that the stilts match.

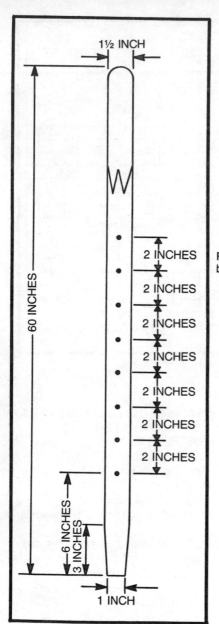

Fig. 6-25. Follow this drawing when boring holes through stilts.

Materials

10 feet of nominal 1¼×2-inch straight grain clear pine
four ⅜×6-inch carriage bolts and wing nuts
two 1-inch rubber crutch tips

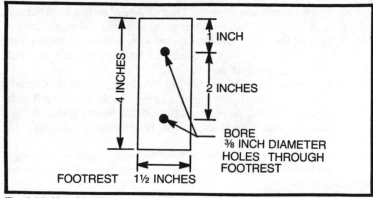

Fig. 6-26. Use this diagram when drilling holes through the stilts' footrests.

two 1½-inch thick scraps of clear pine, each 3½×4 inches
varnish
glue

Construction

1. Cut the 1¼×2-inch board into two 60-inch long pieces. Round off the top ends and taper the bottom ends to 1 inch (Fig. 6-25).

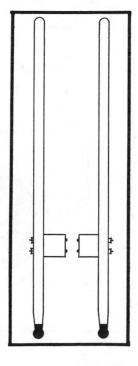

Fig. 6-27. Fasten the footrests to the stilts as shown.

2. Draw a center line down the 1½-inch side of each stilt. Starting 6 inches from the 1-inch wide tapered end, drill a ⅜-inch diameter hole on the center line through the stilt. Drill seven more holes through each stilt, each hole exactly 2 inches up from the center of the previous hole (Fig. 6-25).
3. Cut two footrests, each 3½×4 inches, from 1½-inch thick board. Draw a line down the center of the 1½-inch side. Bore two ¾-inch diameter holes 2 inches apart through the footrests (Fig. 6-26).
4. Sand the stilts smooth and varnish. Glue the rubber crutch tips to the tapered ends.
5. Attach the footrests to the stilts with carriage bolts and wing nuts as illustrated (Fig. 6-27).

CRAWL-IN CUBE

Here is another toy that is particularly suitable for very young children. Use bright colors when painting to make the cube attractive (Fig. 6-28).

Materials

two 4×8 foot and one 4×4 foot sheet of ¾-inch plywood
    or fiberboard
12 feet of 2×2
8d finishing nails
glue
paint

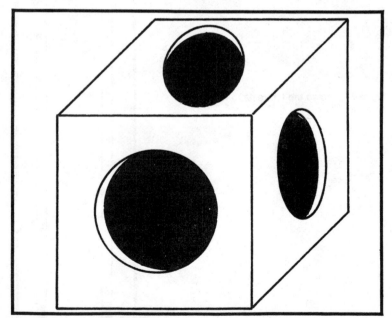

Fig. 6-28. The crawl-in cube makes a nice hiding place.

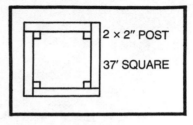

Fig. 6-29. Fasten the 2 by 2 lengths and the 3-foot square in this manner.

2 × 2" POST

37' SQUARE

Construction

1. Cut four 3-foot squares and one 36¾-inch square from the plywood or fiberboard.
2. Cut out a 15-inch diameter circle in the center of each square.
3. Glue and nail the four 3 foot squares together to form a box as illustrated in the assembly diagram.
4. Saw four 3 foot lengths of 2×2. Glue and nail one length in each inside corner of the box (Fig. 6-29).
5. Glue and nail the 36¾-inch square to the top of the box (Fig. 6-29).
6. Paint the inside and outside of the box contrasting colors. Or, paint the five sides different colors.

Puzzles, Blocks, and Games

This chapter is concerned with the construction of various puzzles, blocks and games. Many children enjoy these creations even more than toys. Several of the items described in this section are excellent educational devices. Some games will help your child develop a healthy, competitive attitude. It is never too early to learn about good sportsmanship. All playthings are included because we feel you and your child will enjoy them. For the tiny tot, the stand-up animal puzzles and pre-school puzzles are perfect. Elementary school children will enjoy putting the jigsaw and tangram puzzles together. The seven toys dealing with buildings, blocks and boxes are not difficult. Just be patient when you're sawing, sanding and painting. Projects like the puppet theatre and table football game are more difficult to build than some of the other toys. You may want to ask a friend or relative to assist you.

You parents will have fun making the checkers, chess, tic tac toe and beanbag toss games. The kids might need some expert advice from you on playing the games. We highly recommend that you build the blackboard/ easel. Encourage the children to spend a lot of time using this item constructively. We truly feel that making many of these playthings will be well worth your time. Also, your children will benefit immeasurably.

STAND-UP ANIMAL PUZZLES

Any kind of animal shape makes a nice stand-up puzzle (Fig. 7-1).

Materials

    1 foot of 1×6 for lion
    6 feet of 1×6 for dog

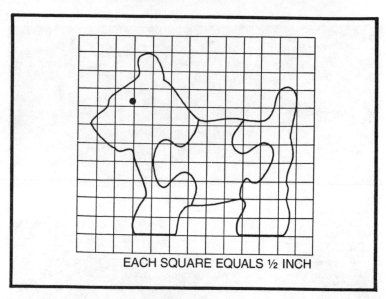

EACH SQUARE EQUALS ½ INCH

Fig. 7-1. Enlarge and trace this dog shape on the wood.

Construction

1. Enlarge Figs. 7-1 and 7-2, and trace them on the wood.
2. Saw out the puzzle. Sand the rough edges.
3. Assemble (Figs. 7-3 through 7-6).

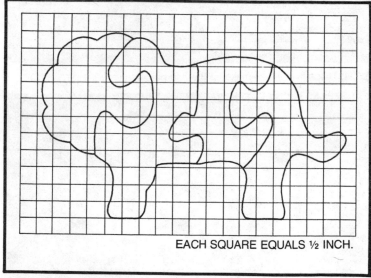

EACH SQUARE EQUALS ½ INCH.

Fig. 7-2. Also enlarge and outline the lion shape.

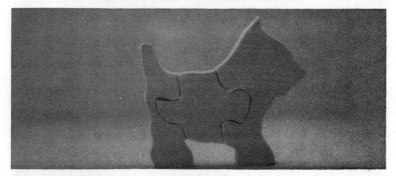

Fig. 7-3. The assembled stand-up dog puzzle.

Fig. 7-4. These five pieces make up the lion puzzle.

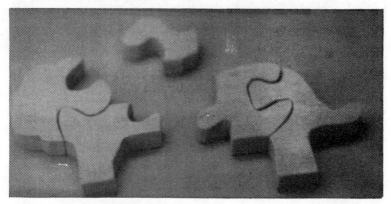

Fig. 7-5. Assemble the pieces as shown.

Fig. 7-6. A completed lion puzzle.

TANGRAM PUZZLE

This is an ancient Chinese puzzle that can be reassembled into many different figures (Fig. 7-7).

Materials

6 inch square of ½-inch thick pine
polyurethane varnish

Construction

1. Trace Fig. 7-8 onto the pine and saw out the pieces.
2. Sand the rough edges.
3. Varnish each piece.

T PUZZLE

The four pieces of this puzzle are surprisingly difficult for a youngster to assemble.

Materials

scrap of ½-inch clear pine, at least 7½×7½ inches
varnish

Construction

1. Trace Fig. 7-9 on the wood and saw out.
2. Sand any rough edges.
3. Varnish each piece.

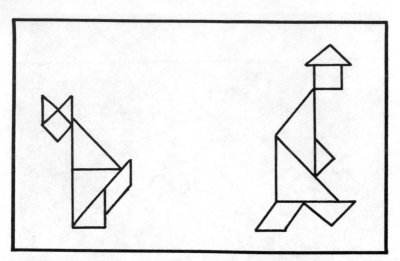

Fig. 7-7. This tangram puzzle can be rearranged into various shapes.

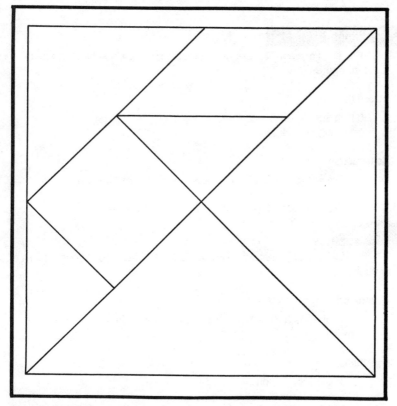

Fig. 7-8. Trace the tangram puzzle pattern on the pine and cut it out.

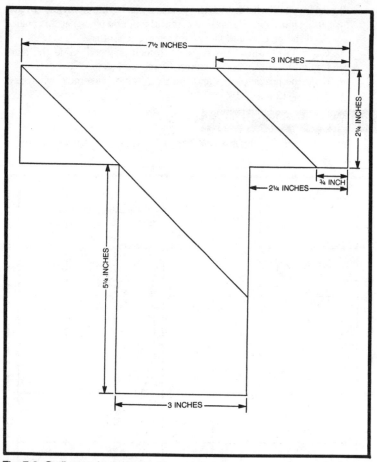

Fig. 7-9. Outline and cut out this T puzzle pattern.

You can find lots of simple designs suitable for puzzles like these in coloring books

Materials

9 inch long piece of ½×12-inch clear pine
scrap of ¼-inch plywood, 9×11¼ inches
glue
paint

Construction

1. Cut a 9×11¼-inch piece of ½-inch pine. Trace Figs. 7-10 and 7-11 on the pine, centering it attractively.

167

2. Drill a small hole through the pine at a place where two lines of the puzzle intersect. Begin sawing out the puzzle pieces at this point. Sand the pieces until all the edges are smooth.

3. Cut a 9×11¼-inch rectangle of ¼-inch plywood. Glue the pine frame to the plywood backing. Clamp until dry.

4. Paint the puzzle pieces and the pine frame. Assemble when dry (Figs. 7-12 and 7-13).

SHAPES AND COLORS PUZZLE

If you have or can obtain an *electric* saber saw, you can cut out these puzzle shapes quickly.

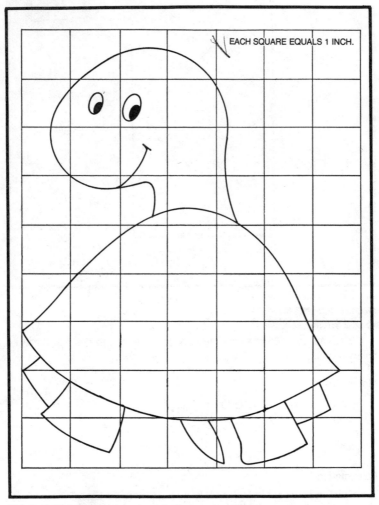

EACH SQUARE EQUALS 1 INCH.

Fig. 7-10. This is the pre-school turtle puzzle pattern.

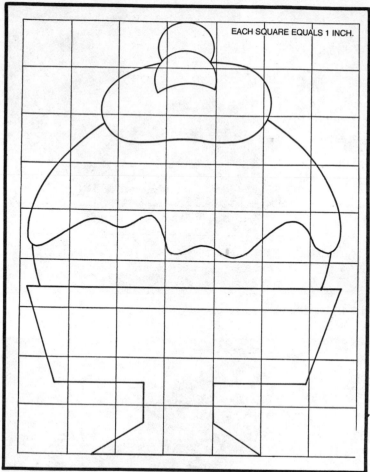

Fig. 7-11. The ice cream sundae puzzle pattern even looks delicious.

Materials

10 inches of 1×8 inch clear pine
scrap of ¼ inch plywood, at least 7¼×10 inches
six beads
glue
brads
red, yellow, blue, green, purple, and orange paint

Construction

1. Following Fig. 7-14, saw out six shapes from the pine board with a saber saw. Sand the edges of the shapes so they can be easily removed from the background.

Fig. 7-12. Paint the turtle puzzle pieces.

Fig. 7-13. The completed pre-school turtle puzzle.

170

2. Cut a 7¼×10-inch rectangle from the ¼-inch plywood. Place the pine frame in position over the plywood backing, and trace the cutout shapes onto the plywood.
3. Paint each cutout piece a different color. Paint the tracings on the plywood to correspond with each puzzle piece.
4. Attach the beads to the center of each shape with a brad.
5. Glue the pine frame to the plywood backing. Clamp until dry. Assemble the puzzle.

JIGSAW PUZZLE

Be creative when designing the puzzle shapes. The list of possibilities is endless.

Materials

poster or art print
¼-inch thick plywood cut the exact size of the print
tracing paper
rubber cement
glue

Construction

1. Glue the print to the plywood.
2. Plan the puzzle on tracing paper. Refer to Fig. 7-15 for examples of puzzle pieces. To personalize the puzzle, design a *few* pieces in specific shapes, such as a car, horse, initials, etc.

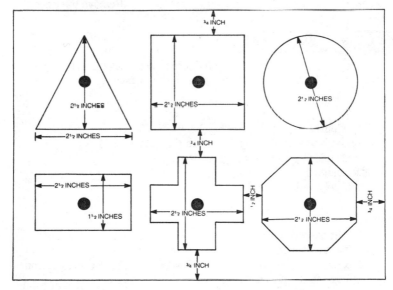

Fig. 7-14. Use a saber saw to cut out these six shapes.

Fig. 7-15. Here are examples of puzzle parts.

3. Glue the tracing paper cutting pattern to the poster with rubber cement. It can be easily removed *if it is not kept on for more than one hour*.
4. Cut out the puzzle pieces with a table jigsaw. Remove the tracing paper and rubber cement.

FRAMED JIGSAW PUZZLE

A framed jigsaw puzzle takes little more time to make than the jigsaw puzzle itself. The frame makes the puzzle more attractive.

Materials

jigsaw puzzle
¼-inch plywood cut the same size as the puzzle
⅛-inch thick by ½-inch wide wood strip
glue, brads
paint, polyurethane varnish

Construction

1. Cut the wood strip into four pieces, two as long as side A of the puzzle, and two ¼-inch longer than side B.
2. Frame the plywood base with the wood strips braded and glued on edge to the plywood (Fig. 7-16).
3. Paint and then varnish.

172

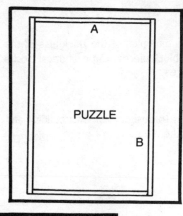

Fig. 7-16. Attach the wood strips to the base as shown.

PUZZLE BLOCKS

These puzzle blocks are delightful playthings on a rainy day.

Materials

Unpainted 1⅜-inch wood cubes (see Color Cubes)
Six paper illustrations
spray adhesive
polyurethane varnish

Construction

1. Arrange the blocks in a square or a rectangle. For an *illustration size,* you will need *number of blocks:*

7×7	25
5½×8¼	24
5½×7	20
5½×5½	16

2. Spray adhesive over the top of the blocks and on the back of one illustration. Press the illustration to the blocks and smooth.
3. When dry, cut through the paper with a matte knife to separate the blocks.
4. Cover the remaining five sides in a similar manner.
5. Coat all sides with polyurethane.

BUILDING BLOCKS

Children do all sorts of things with these blocks. Often they see who can stack the highest tower of blocks without having them collapse.

Materials

Soft pine lumber with a thickness one-half the width, i.e.
   1×2 (actual size ¾×1½) or 1¼×2½ (actual 1 1/16×2⅛)
Dowel with a diameter equal to the thickness of the lumber

Construction

The dimensions of each block are multiples of the thickness of the lumber. Use Fig. 7-17 and saw out the block pieces. Cut cylindrical blocks from the dowel. Sand all the rough edges.

CITY/COUNTRY BUILDING SET

Imaginative youngsters might want to design their own building and tree shapes. All you have to do is cut them out.

Materials

1½-inch thick pine

Construction

1. Outline the building and tree shapes on the pine, and saw out the desired number (Fig. 7-18).
2. Sand smooth.
3. Paint or varnish if you wish.

MOSAIC BLOCKS

Mosaic blocks can be educational devices. You might explain some geometric principles to the kids by using the various shapes.

Materials

12¾-inch square of ¼-inch thick plywood
¼-inch thick clear pine

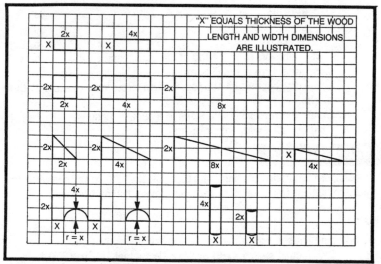

Fig. 7-17. Use these building block patterns.

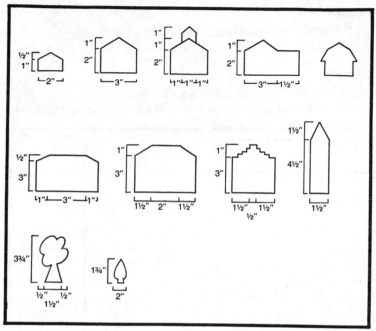

Fig. 7-18. You may trace and cut out as many of these building and tree shapes as you need.

¼-inch pine trim
glue, four brads
primer; red, yellow, blue, and white paint

Construction

1. Using Fig. 7-19 illustrated, saw out the following blocks from the ¼ inch thick pine: ten squares, sixteen triangles, four small rectangles, four large rectangles, and eight rhomboids.
2. Sand any rough edges. Prime. Paint the blocks so that there are four triangles, one small rectangle, one large rectangle, and two rhomboids in each of the four colors. Paint the two remaining squares in whatever colors you wish.
3. Cut the ¼ inch trim into two 12¾-inch lengths and two 12¼ inch lengths. Glue the trim flush with the edges of the plywood square. Brad once at each corner.
4. Prime and then paint the frame.
5. Insert the blocks into the frame (Fig. 7-20).

COLOR CUBES

These six-sided figures will keep the kids entertained for hours. A lot of sawing is necessary. Do the cutting meticulously.

Materials

1½×1½×36 inch wood (actual size 1⅜×1⅜×36 inches)
primer; red, green, yellow, and blue paint

Construction

1. Cut 25 cubes, each 1⅜×1⅜×1⅜ inches.
2. Prime, and when dry, paint as shown in the diagram (Fig. 7-21).

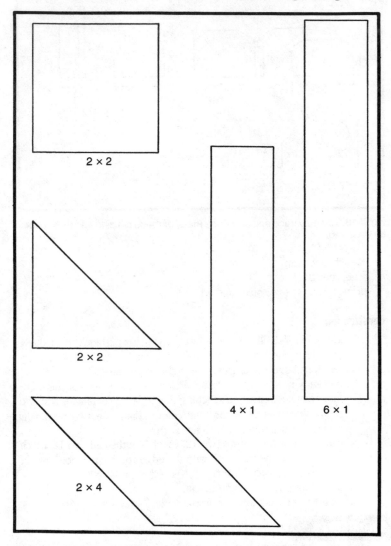

Fig. 7-19. From these patterns trace ten squares, sixteen triangles, four small rectangles, four large rectangles and eight rhomboids. Cut them out of the pine.

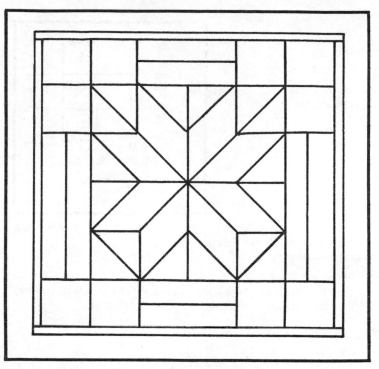

Fig. 7-20. Put the mosaic blocks into the frame as shown.

It will be interesting to see what creations your tots can come up with using these materials.

Materials

3 feet of 1¼-inch diameter pole
12 feet of ¼-inch diameter dowel
3 feet of 1¼×1¼-inch wood strips

Construction

1. 3/16 inches from one end of the 1¼-inch pole, mark and drill three ¼-inch diameter holes ¼-inch deep around the circumference of the pole. ⅝ inches from these holes drill three more, until there are 48 sets of holes down the pole (Fig. 7-22).
2. Cut the 1¼-inch pole into 48 ⅝-inch thick slices so that each slice has three holes around its circumference.
3. Drill a ¼-inch diameter hole through the center of each slice.
4. Cut the strips into 24 1¼-inch cubes. Drill a ¼-inch diameter hole ¼-inch deep in the center of each of the six sides of the cubes.

177

Fig. 7-21. Paint the cubes according to this illustration.

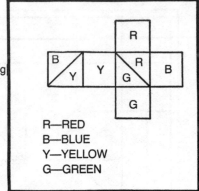

R—RED
B—BLUE
Y—YELLOW
G—GREEN

5. Cut the ¼-inch dowel into twelve 2-inch pieces, twelve 4-inch pieces, and twelve 6-inch pieces.

NEST OF BOXES

The whole neighborhood will love playing with these boxes. You may substitute other colors for the suggested ones if you wish.

Materials

2×4 feet sheet of ¼ inch thick plywood
glue, brads
primer: red, yellow, blue, green paint

Construction

1. Cut out from the plywood:
    for the 4¼-inch box—one 4¼×4¼ inch base
    four 4×4 inch sides;
    for the 3¼-inch box—one 3¼×3¼ inch base
    four 3×3 inch sides;

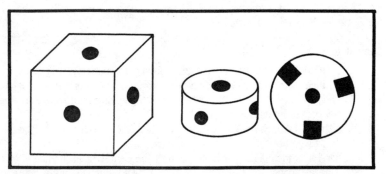

Fig. 7-22. Take pains when boring the holes for the sticks, squares and circles building set.

178

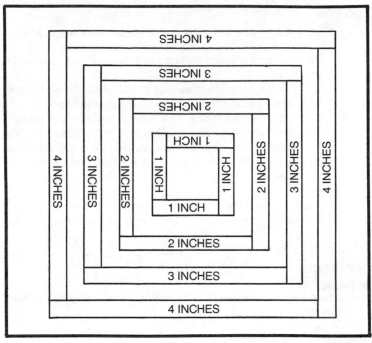

Fig. 7-23. Refer to this diagram when working with the sides and bases for the nest of boxes.

for the 2¼-inch box—one 2¼×2¼ inch base
four 2×2 inch sides;
for the 1¼-inch box—one 1¼×1¼ inch base
four 1×1 inch sides

2. Build all four boxes in the same manner. Glue and brad the sides together, and then glue and brad this frame to the base (Fig. 2-23).

3. Sand any rough edges. Prime. Paint each box a different color.

GAMEBOARD

Make sure to apply a coat of lacquer to the finished gameboard. The finish is hard and immune to many things that would attack other finishes.

Materials

¼-inch thick plywood, 20 inches square
¼ inch thick cork sheeting, at least 12×12×20 inches, in both natural and dark brown colors
7 foot of ¼ inch thick ×½-inch wide wood lattice or finishing strips
glue, brads
wood stain
clear lacquer

Construction

1. With a pencil, draw a 16-inch square in the center of the 20 inch square so that the 16-inch square is 2 inches in from all edges. Divide the 16-inch square into 64 2 inch squares, eight down and eight across.
2. Cut 32 2-inch squares of natural cork and 32 2-inch squares of dark brown cork. Glue the cork squares to the plywood base.
3. Cut two strips of natural cork 2-inches wide by 20-inches long and two strips of dark brown cork 2-inches wide by 20-inches long. To mitre the corners, overlap the border strips at the corners. Place a ruler diagonally across the corner of the square and cut through both strips of cork (Fig. 7-24). Glue the mitred strips to the plywood base.
4. Cut the finishing strips into two 20-inch long pieces and two 20½-inch long pieces. Stain them. Glue and brad these strips on edge to frame the base (Fig. 7-25).
5. Coat the board with a clear lacquer.

CHECKERS

You can make these checkers in just minutes. Then teach your tots how to play the game.

Materials

17 foot of 1¼-inch diameter dowel
primer
red and black paint
polyurethane varnish

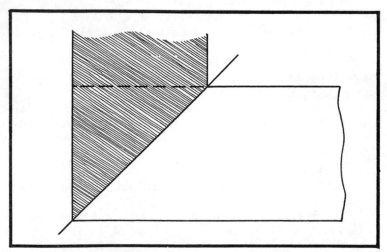

Fig. 7-24. Make sure to place a ruler diagonally across the corner of the square.

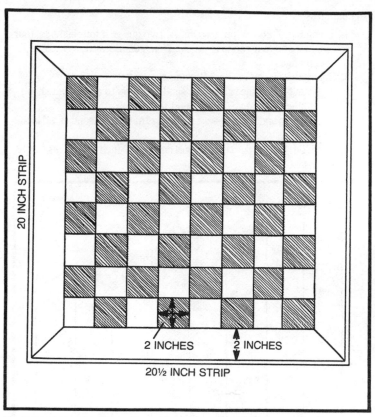

Fig. 7-25. Follow this illustration when dealing with the cork squares and border strips.

Construction

1. Cut the 1¼-inch dowel into 32 ¼-inch thick slices. Sand rough edges.
2. Prime each piece. When dry, paint 16 checkers red and 16 black.
3. Coat each checker with polyurethane.

CHESS SET

Older kids will love this beautiful chess set and will want to play the game constantly. Your kids might develop into grandmasters!

Materials

30 inches of 1-inch diameter dowel
2 feet of ¾-inch diameter dowel
two ⅜-inch beads, two brads
walnut stain, polyurethane varnish

Construction

1. Using Fig. 7-26, cut out two kings, two queens, four bishops, four knights, and four rooks from the 1 inch diameter dowel. Sand the rough edges.
2. Shape the pieces in the following manner:
   King—first file, and then sand the tops to a rounded shape.
   Queen—brad a ⅜-inch bead to the top.
   Bishop and Knight—cut the dowel at the angle indicated in the pattern.
3. From the ¾-inch diameter dowel cut 16 1¼-inch long slices for the pawns.

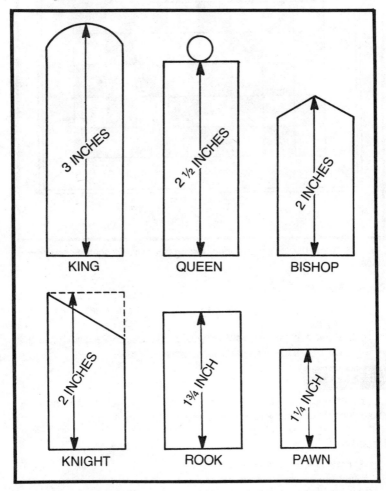

Fig. 7-26. Trace and cut out two kings, two queens, four bishops, four knights and four rooks from the dowel.

4. Stain one set of pieces: one king, one queen, two bishops, two knights, two rooks, and eight pawns.
5. Varnish both sets.

THREE-DIMENSIONAL TIC TAC TOE

The winner is the first to get three circles in a row—vertically, horizontally, or diagonally. This game is for two players (Fig. 7-27).

Materials

6 inches of 1×8-inch pine
15 inches of ½ × 6-inch pine
22 inches of ¼-inch diameter dowel
stain
glue

Construction

1. Cut a 6-inch square from the 1×8 inch pine. Sand the edges smooth.
2. Drill nine ¼-inch diameter, ½-inch deep blind holes in the 6-inch square at the points indicated on Fig. 7-28.
3. Cut nine 2½-inch long pieces of ¼-inch diameter dowel, and glue them in the nine holes of the 6 inch square.
4. From the ½-inch pine cut out 36 1¼ inch diameter circles. Use a hole saw attached to your electric drill to cut them. Enlarge the center hole of each circle to ⅜-inch diameter by drilling through the existing hole with a ⅜-inch bit.
5. Stain 18 circles.

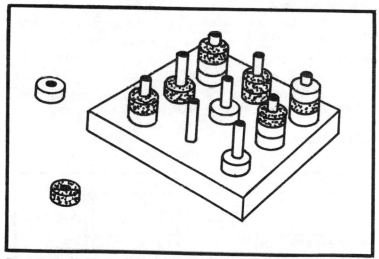

Fig. 7-27. This tic tac toe game can be enjoyed by all members of the family.

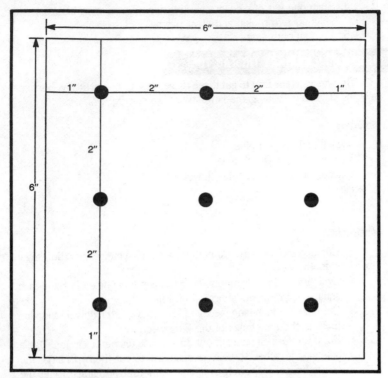

Fig. 7-28. Drill the holes in the square according to this illustration.

TABLE FOOTBALL

Your son can match his favorite National Football League teams against each other with this game.

Materials

2×3 foot sheet of ½ inch A-C interior plywood
15 feet of ¼ inch diameter dowel cut into eight 22 inches long rods
5 feet of ½ inches diameter dowel cut into 22 2¼ inches long "players"
6d finishing nails, glue
paint—three colors, polyurethane varnish

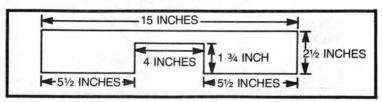

Fig. 7-29. Use this pattern to trace the table football ends.

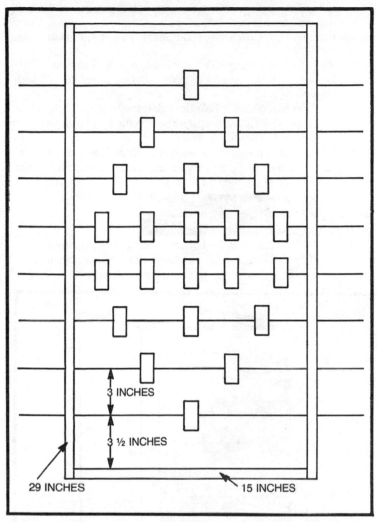

Fig. 7-30. Drill the holes through the table football sides as shown.

Construction

1. Saw out the following pieces from the plywood and sand smooth:
   base—one rectangle 16×29 inches
   ends—two rectangles with cut-outs 2½×15 inches (use Fig. 7-29)
   sides—two rectangles 2½×29 inches.

2. Starting 3½ inches in from one end of a side piece and 1 inch down from the top, mark the drilling point for eight holes every 3 inches. To insure matching holes on the two sides, tape the sides together

and drill the eight 5/16-inch diameter holes through both sides at the same time (Fig. 7-30).

3. Glue and nail the sides to the ends, forming a box. Glue and nail the box to the base.

4. Prime the box and paint whatever color you wish. Paint a contrasting horizontal line across the midpoint of the base. Varnish with polyurethane.

5. Drill a ¼-inch diameter hole through the side of each "player" at the midpoint. Paint eleven players one color and eleven players a second color. Varnish.

6. Put the rods through the holes on one side of the box. Glue the players on the rods so they are arranged like the illustration. Stick the free end of the rods through the holes on the opposite side.

CONVERTIBLE PUPPET THEATRE FOR HAND PUPPETS AND MARIONETTES

Hang the felt curtain over the bottom opening to use the theatre for hand puppets (Fig. 7-31). Hang the curtain over the top opening and push the marionette stage in place to use the theatre for marionettes (Fig. 7-32).

Fig. 7-31. Use the top opening of the theatre for hand puppets.

Fig. 7-32. Use the bottom opening of the theatre for marionettes.

Materials

13½ feet of 1×4-inch pine
10 feet of 1×12-inch pine
4×4 foot sheet of ¼-inch A-D plywood
one cafe curtain rod to cover a 28-inch opening
two sets of mounting brackets for the curtain rod
one package of clip-on cafe curtain rings
six 1¾-inch long machine bolts, ¼ inch×20 inches
six cap nuts to fit the machine bolts
8d finishing nails
duplex head nails
26×28-inch rectangle of felt
felt squares in assorted colors for decorating the curtain
Sobo glue
paint (optional)

Construction

1. Saw the 1×4 inch pine into two 58½-inch vertical uprights, and three 33-inch horizontal bars.
2. Temporarily nail the two verticals and three horizontals together with duplex head nails as illustrated in Fig. 7-33. The two verticals are nailed on top of the three horizontals.

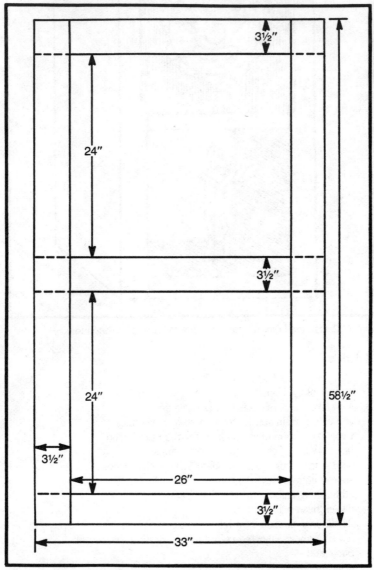

Fig. 7-33. Fasten the two vertical pieces on top of the three horizontal ones.

3. Drill one ¼-inch diameter hole through the horizontal and vertical boards at the six places whre they join. Insert a machine bolt through the boards and fasten with a cap nut (Fig. 7-34). Remove the duplex head nails.

4. Screw the two sets of curtain rod mounts to the vertical boards, one at a point 1½ inches down from the top and the second at the midpoint (Fig. 7-34).

5. Saw the 1×12 inch pine into two 58½-inch lengths. Nail them to either side of the assembled frame, at a 90 degree angle to the vertical boards and flush with them.

6. Build a marionette stage from the plywood. Saw the plywood into the following pieces:

> backdrop—one 26×30 inch rectangle
> stage—one 10¼×26-inch rectangle
> sides—two 9¾×30-inch rectangles.

Assemble the stage as illustrated in Fig. 7-35. To use the stage, push it between the sides of the theatre until the overhang of the stage floor rests on the bottom horizontal board of the theatre front.

7. Decorate a piece of 26×28-inch felt with a felt picture by gluing on the felt pieces with Sobo glue.

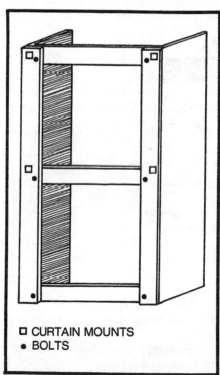

Fig. 7-34. This diagram shows placement of curtain rod mounts and machine bolts.

□ CURTAIN MOUNTS
● BOLTS

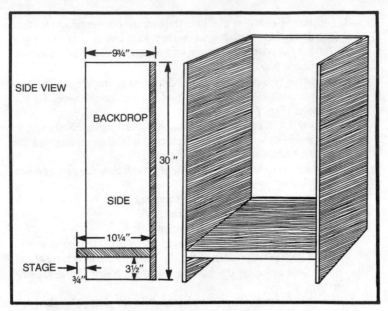

Fig. 7-35. Refer to this illustration for assembling the marionette stage.

8. Clip the curtain rings to the felt, and hang the curtain on the curtain rod.
9. Paint the theatre, if you wish.

DOUBLE-SIDED EASEL/BLACKBOARD

This combination easel/blackboard is perfect for the young artist and student. Just provide your tots with paints, a paint brush, a smock or apron and lots of chalk (Fig. 7-36).

Materials

12 feet of 1×2-inch pine
two 24 inch squares of ⅛-inch hardboard
No. 8×¾-inch screws
1 pair of 3 inch strap hinges with screws
two folding leg brackets with screws
two large paper clamps
blackboard paint

Construction

1. Cut four 36-inch lengths of 1×2-inch pine.
2. Paint one side of each of the hardboard squares with blackboard paint.
3. Screw the hardboard, painted side up, to the wide side of the 1×2 inch legs, as shown in the assembly diagram.

190

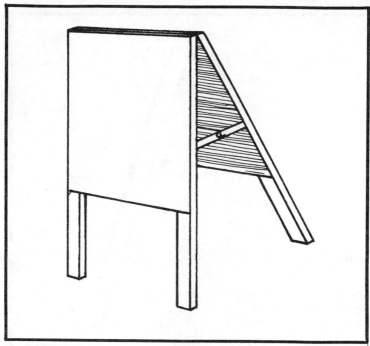

Fig. 7-36. The blackboard/easel is a great learning aid.

4. Join the two assembled panels with strap hinges connecting the top edges of the legs, and with folding leg brackets connecting the side of the legs. Refer to Fig. 7-37.
5. Clip the two paper clamps to the top edge of one panel to hold paper for painting.

TONE BOX

Each of the four sides of this box produces a different sound when you hit it.

Materials

2 feet of ½×12-inch pine
6d finishing nails
1-inch diameter wooden bead
6 inches of ¼-inch diameter dowel
glue

Construction

1. Cut four 6-inch lengths of ½×12-inch pine.
2. Saw a different slit pattern through the thickness of each piece. Center the pattern on the board before you cut (Fig. 7-38).

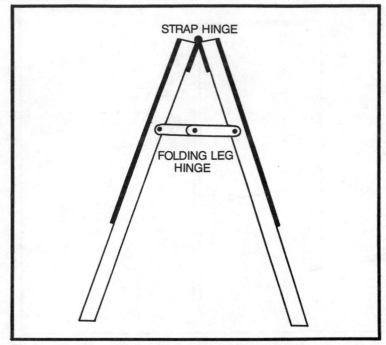

Fig. 7-37. This illustration shows you how to connect the easel legs.

3. Glue and nail the four lengths together as shown in Fig. 7-39.
4. To make a playing stick to hit the box with, drill a ¼-inch diameter hole ¾-inches deep in the wooden bead, and glue a 6 inch length of ¼-inch diameter dowel in the hole.

BEANBAG TOSS

Mom and Dad can work together in making this fun-filled game. Mom can sew the beanbags while Dad does the woodworking.

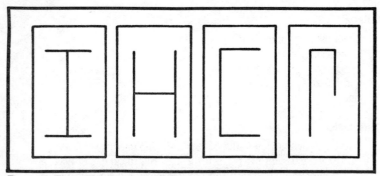

Fig. 7-38. These are tone box slit diagrams.

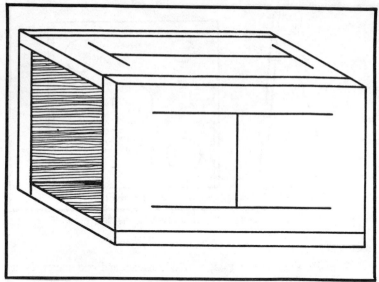

Fig. 7-39. Attach the tone box lengths in this manner.

Materials

    2×3 foot piece of ⅜ inch A-D plywood
    4d finishing nails
    glue
    paint
    scraps of tightly woven fabric or felt
    dried beans

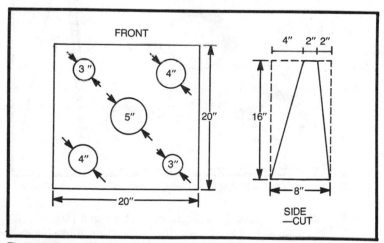

Fig. 7-40. Trace and cut out these beanbag toss game pieces. You will need two sides and one front.

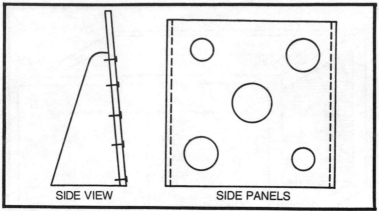

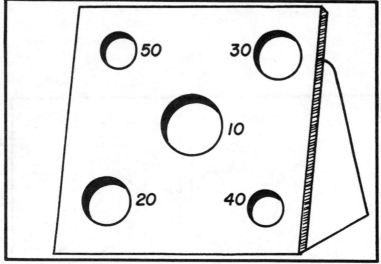

Fig. 7-41. Join the side pieces to the square's back as illustrated.

Construction

1. Using Fig. 7-40, cut out two side pieces and one square front piece. Sand smooth.
2. Glue and nail the side pieces to the back of the square as shown in Fig. 7-41.

Fig. 7-42. Your completed beanbag toss gameboard should look like this one.

3. Paint the board and draw the score numbers on it (Fig. 7-42).
4. Make beanbags by sewing together three sides of two 3½ inch square pieces of fabric, loosely filling the squares with dried beans, and then sewing the open side shut.

Figure Toys

In this fairly brief chapter you will learn how to build figure toys. All of these items can be built out of discarded wood scraps. Always try to save leftover wood. It will come in handy for projects of this nature. For these toys, you will need lots of paint, brads, screws and glue.

Pre-schoolers will be fascinated with the walking man toy. They will probably push the toy up and down the street for hours. The palace guards and guardhouse are beautiful toys that contain intricate details. Robots are not hard to build; they will be the star attractions when the kids play outer space games. The dancing bear and Goldilocks and the three bears are real charmers.

WALKING MAN

The walking man toy has been around for hundreds of years. To make him walk, use the dowel in his back to push him along a flat surface (Fig. 8-1).

Materials

scrap of ½-inch thick wood, at least 2×7 inches
scrap of ⅜-inch thick wood, at least 1×3 inches
scrap of ¼-inch thick wood, at least 2×3 inches
1 foot of ½-inch diameter dowel
1 inch brads

Construction

1. Using Fig. 8-2, saw out one body and two feet from the ½-inch thick wood; two legs from the ⅜-inch thick wood; and two arms from the ¼-inch thick wood. Sand all the pieces smooth.

Fig. 8-1. Use the dowel in the man's back to make him walk.

2. Drill a ½-inch diameter ¼-inch deep blind hole in the back of the body piece. Drill ⅛-inch diameter holes through the arms and legs.
3. Brad the feet to the legs, and the legs and arms to the body.
4. Insert a 12-inch long piece of ½-inch diameter dowel in the hole in the man's back.

PALACE GUARDS

You'll have to have a steady hand to paint the small details on these tiny figures (Fig. 8-3).

Materials

1-inch diameter dowel, 4-inch piece for each guard
¼-inch diameter dowel, 3½-inch piece for each guard
scrap of ¼-inch thick plywood, at least 12×12 inches
one No. 4×1-inch flathead screw for each guard
brads
glue
paint

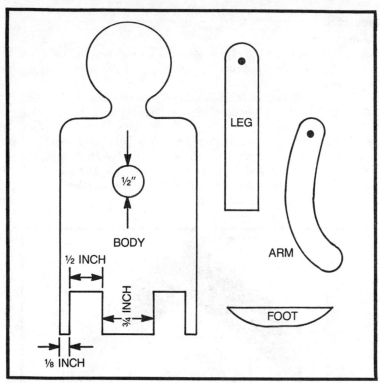

Fig. 8-2. Here are the patterns for tracing one body and two feet on the ½-inch thick wood, two legs on the ⅜-inch wood, and two arms on the ¼-inch wood.

Fig. 8-3. The palace guard and guardhouse require meticulous painting.

Construction

Guards

1. For each guard you plan to make cut a 4-inch long piece of 1-inch diameter dowel and two 1¾-inch long pieces of ¼-inch diameter dowel.
2. Round off one end of the 1-inch dowel with a file. Sand smooth. Drill a 1/16-inch diameter hole ¼-inch deep in the center of the flat end of the dowel.
3. Round off one end of each piece of ¼-inch diameter dowel.
4. Cut a 1½-inch diameter circle base out of the ¼-inch plywood. Use a hole saw attached to an electric drill to do this. Drill a 7/64-inch diameter hole through the center of the circle, and then countersink for a No. 4 flathead screw.

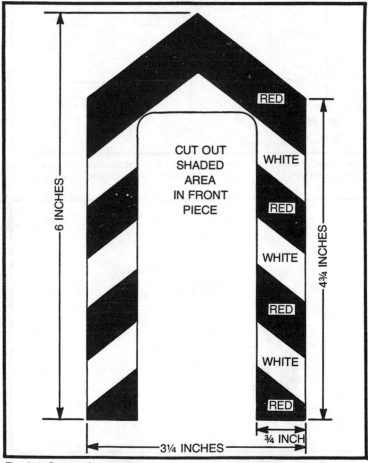

Fig. 8-4. Cut out the guardhouse's front and back carefully.

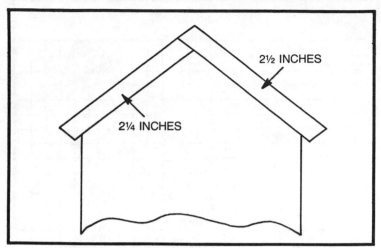

Fig. 8-5. This figure gives you the dimensions and positioning of the roof.

5. Paint the body, arms, and base.
6. Brad the arms to the body. Screw the base to the soldier using the predrilled holes.

Guardhouse

7. Cut out the following pieces from the ¼-inch plywood:
   base—one rectangle, 2×3¼ inches
   sides—two rectangles, 1½×4–¾ inches
   front and back—two pieces 3¼×6 inches (use Fig. 8-4)
   roof—two rectangles, one 2×2¼ inches and one 2×2½ inches (Fig. 8-5).
8. Glue and brad the front and back to the sides, and then, the base to the four walls. Glue and brad the roof on last (Fig. 8-5).
9. Prime, and then paint white with red stripes.

ROBOTS

Building these robots is a good way to use odd pieces of wood and dowel left over from other woodworking projects. Figures 8-6 and 8-7 are meant to be an inspiration for your own imagination, rather than a strict guide. Glossy enamel, metallic paints, and colored tape will make the figures "out-of-this-world."

Materials

wood scraps
dowel pieces
glue
assortment of brads and screws
paint

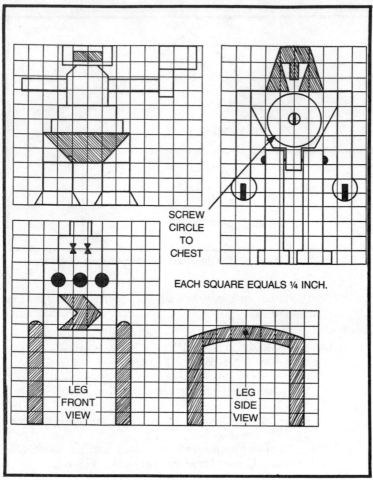

SCREW
CIRCLE
TO
CHEST

EACH SQUARE EQUALS ¼ INCH.

LEG
FRONT
VIEW

LEG
SIDE
VIEW

Fig. 8-6. This illustration shows you how the robots should look.

Construction

1. Using Figs. 8-6 and 8-7 as a guide, cut blocks and circles from the wood scraps to form the various components of the robots. The robots can be made in the sizes illustrated, or can be enlarged by ruling larger squares (½ or 1 inch) on plain paper and then transferring the designs.
2. Glue, brad, and screw the pieces together.
3. Paint (Fig. 8-8).

DANCING BEAR

This little creature will be a star with the very young set. When you fasten the arms and legs, wrap the string securely (Fig. 8-9).

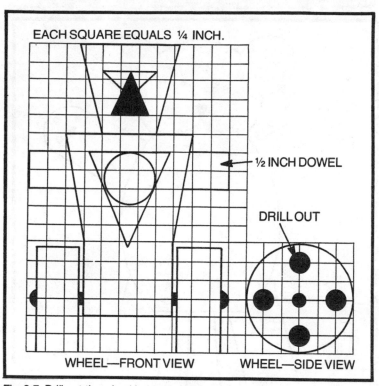

EACH SQUARE EQUALS ¼ INCH.

½ INCH DOWEL

DRILL OUT

WHEEL—FRONT VIEW　　WHEEL—SIDE VIEW

Fig. 8-7. Drill out the wheel holes slowly.

Fig. 8-8. The robot is ready for action.

Fig. 8-9. A completed dancing bear.

Materials

scrap of ¾-inch thick pine
scrap of ½-inch thick pine
four No. 6×¾ inch roundhead screws
upholstery tacks
string

Construction

1. Cut the bear's body from the ¾-inch thick pine, and the arms and legs from ½-inch thick pine (Fig. 8-10). Sand smooth.
2. Drill a 3/16-inch diameter hole through the arms and legs at the points indicated on the cutting diagrams.
3. Tap an upholstery tack into the thickness of each arm and leg as illustrated in Fig. 8-11.

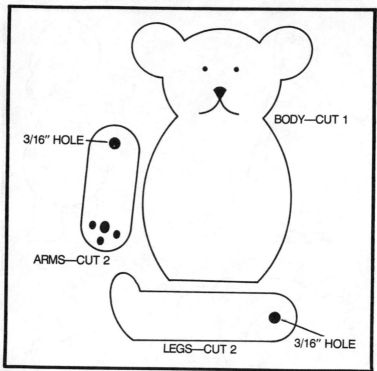

Fig. 8-10. Cut the bear's body from ¾-inch thick pine and the arms and legs from ½-inch thick pine.

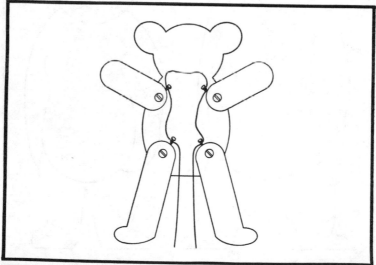

Fig. 8-11. Pound the tacks carefully into the arms and legs.

Fig. 8-12. The Goldilocks and three bears cutting pattern.

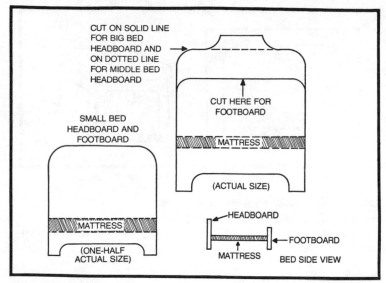

Fig. 8-13. Follow this illustration when you're cutting out and assembling the bed pieces.

4. Use a ball point pen with indelible ink to outline the bear's features.
5. Screw the arms and legs to the body.
6. String the arms and legs together, wrapping the string around the tacks.

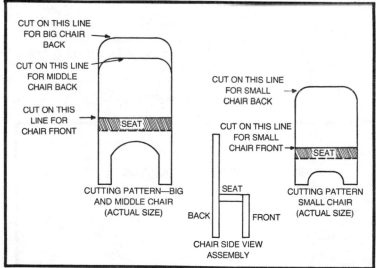

Fig. 8-14. Refer to this diagram when you're cutting out and assembling the chair pieces.

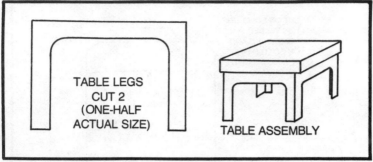

Fig. 8-15. This drawing explains how to cut out and assemble the table pieces.

Your youngsters can re-enact the famous fairy tale using these wooden figures.

Materials

18 inches of 1×4-inch pine
2 feet of ¼×12-inch pine or plywood scrap
small scraps of 1 inch, ¾ inch, and ½ inch diameter dowels
1 inch brads
glue
paint

Construction

1. Trace the three bears and Goldilocks figures on the 1×4-inch pine and saw out (Fig. 8-12). Sand smooth. Paint the features.
2. Cut out the following pieces from the ¼-inch wood and sand smooth (see Figs. 8-13 through 8-15):
   big bed—one headboard, one footboard, and
         one 2¾×6-inch mattress rectangle

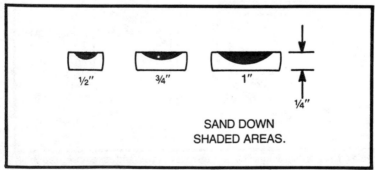

Fig. 8-16. Make a bowl of porridge for each bear.

middle bed—one headboard, one footboard, and
one 2¾×4-inch mattress rectangle

big chair—one back, one front, and one 1×1½-inch
seat rectangle

middle chair—one back, one front, and one
1×1-inch seat rectangle

small chair—one back, one front, and one ¾×1¼-inch
seat rectangle

table—two legs, and one 2½×2½-inch square top.

3. Glue and nail the table, chairs, and beds together as shown in Figs. 8-13 through 8-15.

4. To make bowls of porridge, cut a ¼-inch slice of 1-inch dowel, ¾-inch dowel, and ½-inch dowel. Sand the center of each to create a hollow as shown in Fig. 8-16.

5. Paint the furniture.

Functional Toys

Parents will probably appreciate this final chapter more than any other in the book. The section describes materials needed and directions for making functional or useful toys. In other words, each of these objects has a meaningful purpose other than just pure entertainment or enjoyment. The toys are designed to help children do things and, in some cases, to help remind them of such chores.

Kids can use the bookends, chest, cart, stand and holders to keep track of their prized possessions (books, toys, clothes, pencils, rings). The step stool will get your children off the ground in necessary situations. Nameplates will let them tell the world who they are. A sandbox may keep the children out of mischief.

We hope you'll be eager to make some of these items after reading this introduction. We think you'll be glad you did. Have fun!

BEAR BOOKENDS

These book holders make cute decorations for your child's room.

Materials

    2 feet of 1×6 inch clear pine
    12 inch square of felt
    glue
    8d finishing nails
    paint

Construction

1. Enlarge Fig. 9-1, transfer to the pine, and cut out two bears. Sand smooth.

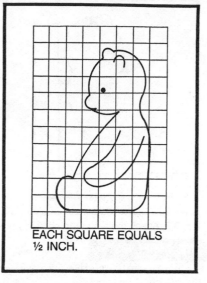

Fig. 9-1. Enlarge and trace the bear bookend pattern on pine. Cut out two bruins.

EACH SQUARE EQUALS ½ INCH.

2. Also saw out four 4½×5-inch rectangles. Sand smooth.
3. Nail the rectangles together to form two L-shaped bookends (Fig. 9-2).
4. Glue and nail one bear to each bookend.
5. Prime and paint.
6. Glue a 4½×5-inch piece of felt to the bottom of each bookend (Fig. 9-3).

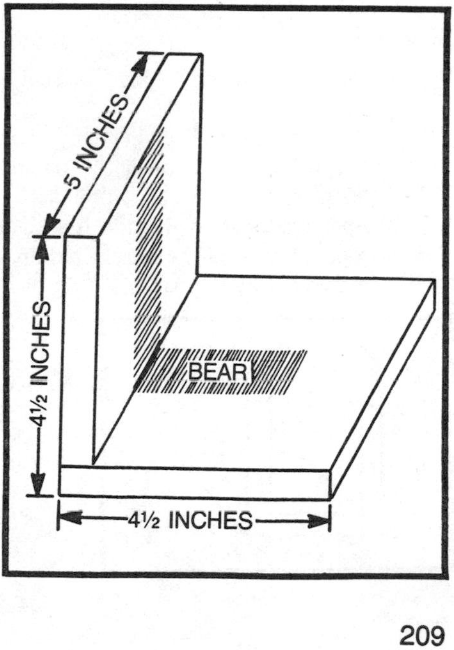

Fig. 9-2. Fasten the bookends as shown.

5 INCHES

4½ INCHES

BEAR

4½ INCHES

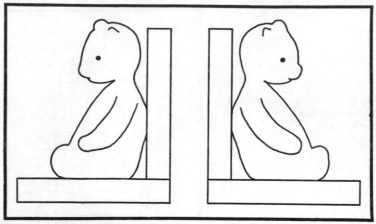

Fig. 9-3. Attach the felt to the bookend bottoms as illustrated.

OWL BOOKENDS

If your child is a bird fancier, you might build a pair of owl bookends. Use durable metal bookends.

Materials

one pair of office-type metal bookends (Fig. 9-4)
1 foot of 1×10-inch clear pine
12-inch square of felt
glue
wood stain

Construction

1. Outline the owl on the pine, and cut out two owls (Fig. 9-5). Sand smooth.
2. With a 1-inch spade bit in your electric drill, drill shallow holes for the owl's eyes. Scratch the outlines of the nose, wings, and feathers into the wood with a nail.
3. Apply stain to the owls on both sides, let it sit for a minute, and then wipe off most of the stain. Darker stain will remain in the lines etched out by the nail.

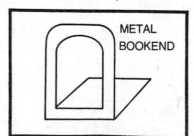

METAL
BOOKEND

Fig. 9-4. Use a pair of metal bookends similar to this one when constructing owl bookends.

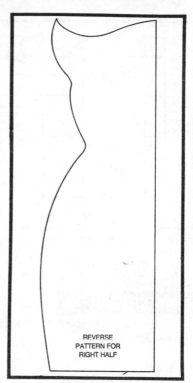

Fig. 9-5. Trace this owl pattern on the pine and cut out two owls.

REVERSE
PATTERN FOR
RIGHT HALF

4. Cut two pieces of felt, each 1-inch wider and twice as long as the vertical upright of the metal bookend. Fold each in half to make it the same length as the upright, and then stitch the two long sides closed. Glue one to the center bottom of the back of each owl so

Fig. 9-6. These owl bookends are very pretty.

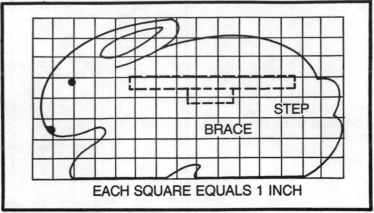

EACH SQUARE EQUALS 1 INCH

Fig. 9-7. Enlarge this rabbit step stool pattern and carefully trace it on the pine.

that the opening in the felt bag is at the bottom. Slip the bag over the upright portion of the metal bookend (Fig. 9-6).

RABBIT STEP STOOL

Your child will be able to reach for things in high places with the help of this beautiful toy.

Materials

4 feet of 1×12-inch pine
8d finishing nails, glue
paint, varnish

Construction

1. Enlarge Fig. 9-7, transfer to the pine, and cut out two rabbits. Sand smooth.
2. Also saw out from the pine one 8×11¼-inch rectangle for the step and one 2×11¼-inch rectangle for the brace. Sand the 11¼-inch edges of the step piece until they are no longer sharp.
3. Glue and nail the 2-inch brace to the center of the step piece.
4. Glue and nail the step and brace between the two rabbits (Fig. 9-8).
5. Prime, paint, and varnish (Figs. 9-9 and 9-10).

TOY CHEST

Do your kids always leave their toys around the house where someone might fall over them? This toy might help them break the habit.

Materials

4×8 foot sheet of ¾-inch A-C interior plywood
8d finishing nails, glue

Fig. 9-8. Glue the step between the rabbits carefully.

30-inch piano hinge and screws
16-inch lid support
four flat-plate swivel casters and mounting screws
paint, varnish

Construction

1. Cut out from the ¾-inch plywood:
    front and back—two rectangles 15×30 inches
    ends—two rectangles 15×16½ inches
    lid—one rectangle 16½×30 inches

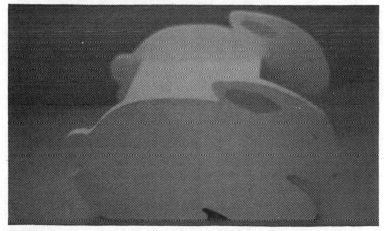

Fig. 9-9. Your completed rabbit step stool should look similar to this one.

Fig. 9-10. This little girl is delighted with her new toy.

        lid rail—one strip 1½×30 inches
        base—one rectangle 16½×28½ inches.

2. Cut out hand holes in the two end panels and the lid. To do this, first bore two 1-inch diameter holes with centers 2½ inches apart and 2 inches in from the edge. Saw out the wood between the holes to complete the hand hole. Sand smooth.

3. Glue and nail the front and back to the ends.

4. Fit the base in the chest so that it is flush with the bottom edges of all four sides. Glue and nail the base to the front, ends, and back.

5. Position the lid rail flush with the back and extending ¾ inch onto either side edge. Glue and nail in place.

6. Lay the lid on top of the chest flush with the lid rail, and screw the piano hinge to both pieces.

7. Screw the 16-inch chain lid support to the inside of the lid top and the right end of the chest.

8. Prime, paint and varnish (Fig. 9-11).

9. Mount the casters on the bottom of the base.

CLOTHES STAND

Here is another handy toy for the sloppy youth. After you complete this toy, there will be no excuse for your child leaving his room cluttered with clothes.

Materials

3 feet of 2×2-inch pine
3 feet of 1 inch diameter dowel
1 foot of 2×12-inch pine
8d finishing nails
glue
paint

Construction

1. Cut a 3-foot long piece of 2×2. Insert the drill bit at a 45 degree angle to the 2×2, and drill one 1-inch diameter 1-inch deep blind hole in each of the four 1½-inch sides of the 2×2 so that there are four holes in all. Drill the first hole 12 inches down from one end; the second hole 9 inches down from the same end; the third, 6 inches down; and the fourth, 3 inches down from one end; the second hole 9 inches down from the same end; the third, 6 inches down; and the fourth, 3 inches down (Fig. 9-12).

Fig. 9-11. A completed toy chest.

215

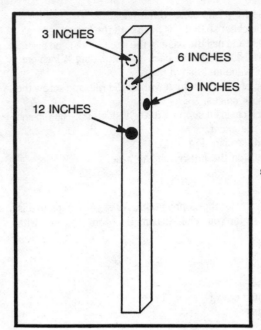

3 INCHES

6 INCHES

9 INCHES

12 INCHES

Fig. 9-12. Bore the clothes stand holes slowly.

2. From the 2×12-inch pine cut out one 8½-inch diameter circle, one 2-inch diameter circle, and four 1½-inch diameter circles. Drill a 1 inch diameter ¾ inches deep blind hole in the center of the four 1½-inch circles.

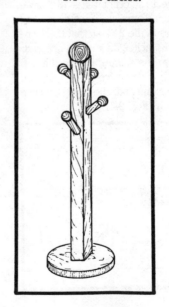

Fig. 9-13. Make sure to attach the small circle to the stand top.

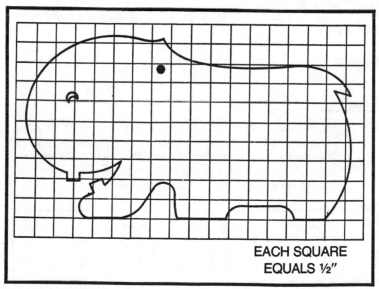

Fig. 9-14. Pencils and pens will never get lost if they are always kept in the holder.

3. Paint the circles and the 2×2 stand different colors.
4. Glue and nail the plain end of the 2×2 to the center of the large circle.
5. Cut four 7-inch long pieces of 1-inch diameter dowel. Glue one end of a 7-inch piece of dowel in one small circle, and the opposite end in the stand. Do the same with the other three circles.
6. Glue the 2-inch circle to the top of the stand (Fig. 9-13).

HIPPO HOLDER

Use this amusing hippo figure to hold pencils, pens, or crayons (Fig. 9-14).

EACH SQUARE EQUALS ½"

Fig. 9-15. Enlarge and transfer this hippo pattern to pine. Saw out.

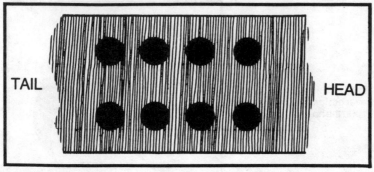

TAIL HEAD

Fig. 9-16. This diagram shows where to drill holes in the holder.

Materials

1 foot of 2×6-inch pine
paint or varnish (optional)

Construction

1. Enlarge Fig. 9-15, transfer it to the pine, and cut out one hippo figure. Sand smooth.
2. Drill eight 5/16 inch diameter holes 1-inch deep into the top of the hippo's back. Refer to Fig. 9-16 for placement.
3. Paint or varnish if you wish.

NAMEPLATE

Stand this on a desk or chest, or hang it on the door of a child's room (Fig. 9-17).

Materials

1½×4-inch pine

Construction

1. Outline the letters of the name you wish to cut out on the pine. Make each letter approximately 2 inches wide and 3½ inches tall—the width of the pine board. Draw the letters of the name so that each letter touches another (Fig. 9-18).
2. Cut out the name with a saber saw equipped with a scroll blade.

Fig. 9-17. Your children will be proud to display their own personal nameplates.

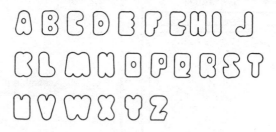

ABCDEFGHIJ
KLMNOPQRST
UVWXYZ

Fig. 9-18. Here are examples of block letters. Be sure that each letter of the name touches another.

3. Bore ¾-inch diameter holes for the openings in letters A,B,D,O,P,Q, and R with a ¾-inch spade bit attached to an electric drill.
4. Sand smooth. Paint or varnish if you wish.

TOY STORAGE CART

Instead of making the chest you might prefer building this cart. Both toys serve the same purpose and are about equal in difficulty to construct (Fig. 9-19).

Materials

6 feet of 1×12-inch pine
7 inches of 1×4-inch pine
16½-inch square of ¾-inch plywood
8d finishing nails
four flat-plate swivel casters and mounting screws
paint or varnish (optional)

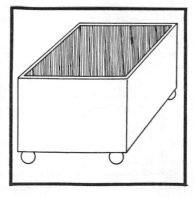

Fig. 9-19. The casters attached to the cart help it move with ease.

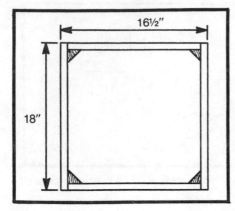

Fig. 9-20. Assemble the cart's side pieces as illustrated.

Construction

1. Cut the 1×12-inch pine into two 18-inch long pieces and two 16½-inch pieces.
2. Nail the two 16½-inch long pieces to opposite sides of the 16½-inch square plywood bottom (Fig. 9-20).
3. Nail the two 18-inch sides to the remaining sides of the plywood square and to the other two side pieces (Fig. 9-20).
4. Cut four isosceles triangles from the 1×4-inch pine. Each triangle should have two sides 3½ inches long. Refer to the Fig. 9-21.
5. Nail one triangular block to each inside corner of the bottom of the box.
6. Screw casters to the bottom of the cart so that they are screwed through the bottom and into the corner blocks.
7. Paint the cart if you wish.

RING HOLDER

This unique toy is best suited for the older child. Take time to cut the dowel pieces with correct dimensions (Fig. 9-22).

Materials

15 inches of ⅜-inch diameter dowel
5 inches of 1×3
glue

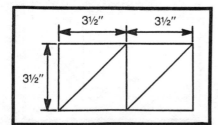

Fig. 9-21. This diagram illustrates how the cart's corner blocks are cut.

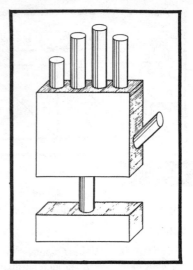

Fig. 9-22. The ring holder has pegs for each finger of the hand.

Construction

1. Cut two 2½-inch squares from the 1×3-inch pine.
2. Drill a ⅜-inch diameter, ½-inch deep blind hole in the center of one square. This square will form the base.
3. In the second square, which will form the palm, drill four ⅜-inch diameter, ½-inch deep blind holes in a ¾-inch edge. In an adjoining edge drill a ⅜-inch diameter, ½-inch edge. In an adjoining edge drill a ⅜-inch diameter, ½-inch deep blind hole at a 45 degree angle. In the edge opposite the edge with the four holes, drill a ⅜-inch diameter, ½-inch deep blind hole in the center.
4. Cut the ⅜-inch dowel into the following pieces and glue them in their respective holes in the palm:

> pinkie—2 inches
> ring finger—2¾ inches
> middle finger—3 inches
> index finger—2⅞ inches
> thumb—1¾ inches
> wrist—2 inches.

5. Glue the other end of the wrist dowel into the hole in the base.

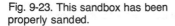
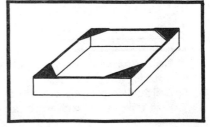

Fig. 9-23. This sandbox has been properly sanded.

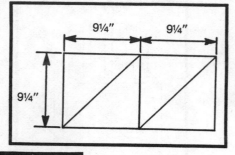

Fig. 9-24. Cut out the sandbox seats according to this illustration.

Every child enjoys playing in a sandbox. This one will give the kids ample space. Now all that's needed is the sand (Fig. 9-23).

Materials

18 feet of 1×10-inch pine
4×4 foot sheet of ¼-inch hardboard
8d finishing nails
wood preservative
paint or stain (optional)

Construction

1. Cut four 47¼-inch long lengths from the 1×10-inch pine.
2. Cut four isosceles triangles from the 1×10-inch pine. Each triangle should have two equal sides, each 9¼ inches long. Refer to Fig. 9-24.
3. Take special pains to sand the hypotenuse of the triangles smooth so that the children sitting on them won't get splinters.
4. Nail the four lengths of pine together to form the sides of the sandbox. Use Fig. 9-25 as a guide.

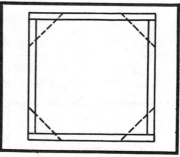

Fig. 9-25. Fasten the sandbox sides together as shown.

5. Nail one triangle to the topside of each corner of the sandbox sides, matching up right angles.
6. Nail the 4×4 foot sheet of hardboard to the bottom of the sandbox.
7. Coat the sandbox with wood preservative. Stain or paint if you wish.

Index